FAITH AROUND THE BARBECUE

(The story)

(Also available as a play)

Phil Ridden

EDWEST PUBLISHING

Copyright © Phil Ridden, 2020

Published 2020 by Edwest Publishing
Joondalup, Western Australia
www.edwestpublishing.biz

ISBN: Paperback 978-0-6488999-1-4

The author asserts his moral rights.
No part of this publication may be reproduced or transmitted, in any form or by any means without the permission of the author, except for fair use in worship and study.

To contact the author:
Phil@philridden.biz
www.philridden.biz

Bible translations quoted

Scripture quotations marked **NIV** are taken from The Holy Bible: New International Version®, NIV® Copyright © 1973, 1978, 1984, 2011 by Biblica, Inc.® Used by permission. All rights reserved worldwide.

Scripture quotations marked **GNT** are taken from Good News Translation® (Todays English Version, Second Edition), Copyright © 1992 American Bible Society. All rights reserved.

Scripture quotations marked **MSG** are taken from The Message. Copyright © 1993, 1994, 1995, 1996, 2000, 2001, 2002. Used by permission of NavPress Publishing Group.

Scripture quotations marked **TLB** are from *The Living Bible* copyright © 1971 by Tyndale House Foundation. Used by permission of Tyndale House Publishers Inc., Carol Stream, Illinois 60188. All rights reserved.

Dedication

As always, this book is dedicated to Kylie. It is also dedicated to all the Christian folk in congregations where I have led worship from time to time.

I offer my sincere appreciation to my daughter, Julie, and my friend and colleague, Pastor Phil Bryant, for their valuable suggestions.

It is written for all who want to understand faith more clearly, follow Christ more surely, and serve God more faithfully.

TABLE OF CONTENTS

INTRODUCTION 1
THE CHARACTERS 2

BECAUSE GOD KNOWS US … CHRISTMAS IS MORE THAN A PARTY 3

    MYSTERY 4
    SOAP OPERA 12
    POLITICS 16
    ROAD TRIP 19
    BABY 24
    SHEPHERDS 29
    CONCERT 33
    WISE MEN 39
    SANTA 44
    SEQUEL 48

BECAUSE GOD WANTS A RELATIONSHIP WITH US … WE MEET HIM IN PERSON, NOT JUST ONLINE 51

    MEETING 52
    BOUNDARIES 57
    MOVING IN 61
    RELATIONSHIPS 67
    SEQUEL 2 71

BECAUSE GOD LOVES US … EASTER IS MORE THAN A HEART EMOJI 72

    LIMB 73
    LITIGATION 80
    HEROES 85
    WOOING 92
    COMMITMENT 97
    LOVE 101

BECAUSE GOD WANTS TO HELP US … HE GIVES US A SUPPORT CREW 105

    FAMILY 106
    CELEBRATIONS 113
    WORDS 122
    HEAVEN 129

BECAUSE GOD IS GOD ... FAITH IS MORE THAN HOPING FOR MAGIC 131

    IN CHARGE..132
    MAKE IT COUNT 140
    CONCLUSION 142

INTRODUCTION

I am not a theologian. I am a Christian who tries to make sense of the world in the context of my faith and to make sense of my faith in the context of the world.

Some people make an academic study of Christianity, but in their pursuit of deeper understanding, they sometimes complicate things.

I believe God wants to be understood — and loved — by everyone, across all time and places and cultures. Jesus came to all, spoke to any who would listen, and left his message in the hands of a group of ordinary people. He still speaks to any who will listen.

So let me explain Christianity, simply and with a little humour, especially to those of you who are confused or just a little unsure. I'll try to explain it as we might do with a group of friends around the barbecue.

THE CHARACTERS

James and Mei: A couple who love talking about their faith. James is very articulate, but he likes to put a humorous twist on things. Mei is more serious, but accepts James' quirkiness. They run an engineering business together, something to do with cranes. (When we meet people, we always seem to want to know what they do for a living. So there you are.)

Ani and Nathan: Both are cynical about Christians — present company excepted. They've seen the hypocrisy of the church, listened to brow-beating Christians, and are generally unimpressed by the whole notion of faith. Ani runs an online business marketing a range of products. Nathan is a vet.

Jo and Alex: They attend church from time to time. Jo would probably like to be more involved, but Alex is unsure. Jo is a teacher. Alex is a courier driver.

Ellie and Pete (me): Ellie is smart and a great conversationalist. She is not embarrassed about asking questions, and she often seems to cut through to the heart of an issue when the rest of us are trying to rationalise everything. I'm not sure I know who I am. Ellie says I try too hard to be funny, and as a result, I am sometimes flippant when I should be serious. She's probably right. I'm pretty sure I'm a Christian, but there's a lot I don't understand. Ellie is a health and safety consultant and I'm a mechanic.

All of us have kids, of various ages. Later on, you will meet our daughter, Gabby. She has been raised in the church, and has kept her faith through the challenges of university. She has recently acquired a boyfriend, Arun. They are both students.

BECAUSE GOD KNOWS US ... CHRISTMAS IS MORE THAN A PARTY

Christmas is loved by people all over the world. It's a season of excesses: over-spending, over-worrying, over-eating, over-indulging, and eventually over it! Some shops display nativity tableaux among the Christmas bargains. Images of Mary, Joseph, baby Jesus, shepherds, wise men and various farm animals pop up on Christmas cards, competing with snow and reindeer, or the jolly, white-bearded, fat man — Santa, of course, not great-grand-dad! What is the relevance of such things to Christmas?

If the Christmas story has a God connection, then what was God thinking? It's simple really.

The wonderful thing about Christmas is that it celebrates how well God knows us.

Let me show you.

MYSTERY

December 22: Around the barbecue at Ani and Nathan's home. A spectacular West Australian summer evening. Drinks and nibbles.

As a group of friends, we are very comfortable with each other. Even Ani and Nathan's two big black Labradors and Russian Blue cat are relaxed around us, mostly ignoring us, unless there is a tummy rub or cuddle on offer.

As we sat around the big wooden table, we chatted about all sorts of things. Somehow the conversation drifted to magicians. Well, to be fair, it didn't really drift. Ellie had seen a magician in the city and videoed him with her phone. She was keen to show it to others, beginning with Ani and Mei who were seated either side of her.

Nathan was curious about why they were huddled over the small screen. 'What are you looking at?'

Ellie spoke without taking her eyes off her phone. 'I saw an illusionist in the city the other day, and he was amazing, so I filmed him.'

'You have to see this.' Ani leaned in for a better view of the small screen, while Jo moved to stand behind Ellie and look over her shoulder. 'I'm always fascinated by the way they somehow trick us into believing the impossible is possible.'

Mei leaned in from the other side of Ellie. 'I know what you mean. In our logical, explainable world, we have a fascination for things we can't explain.'

'I guess we just like mysteries, don't we?' said Alex.

'True — like science fiction or the paranormal,' Nathan added.

'Or why turning a car's ignition off and on again fixes a computer glitch.' I am experienced mechanic who can diagnose and repair mechanical faults, but the workings of the car's computer are a mystery to me.

'Or Christmas.' James off-hand comment surprised everyone.

'Eh?' Ellie looked up. 'Nothing mysterious about Christmas. Same decorations put up in the same way every year. Same bottle of perfume from Pete every year…'

'Burnt roast dinner,' I interjected. Then, seeing Ellie's glare, I quickly added, 'Just joking. I love the treats you like to cook for Christmas.'

James persisted — fortunately. 'Christmas is a fantastic mystery.' He pulled at his ear. I don't know why. He just does that sort of thing a lot.

'How so?' Nathan tilted back his head to drop some peanuts into his mouth.

'Christmas shows how well God knows us.'

'You've lost me.'

'Ah,' said James.

'Because God knows us, he knows that we love a good mystery, so Christmas begins with two mysteries.'

'What mysteries? How fat Santa fits down a narrow chimney?' Alex used his hands to help him ask the question. He tends to do that. Fortunately, he doesn't say much, but when he does, it's risky to be too near his waving arms.

'Or how he breaks into homes that don't have chimneys.' Ellie handed the phone to Alex to watch. 'That's a bit spooky.'

James laughed, but continued unfazed. 'Mystery one is that God became human and lived on earth as Jesus.'

Ani screwed up her face. 'I struggle to comprehend the notion of God living on earth as a man, like an undercover cop. Even setting aside the practicalities, why would God want to be one of us?'

'I agree,' said Nathan. 'If you believe in God, then, by definition, God is above humanity. He reigns, he rules, he oversees, he monitors. He sets the expectations and watches while people struggle to achieve them. He doesn't get intimately involved.'

'Just zaps them when they get it wrong and lets them win Lotto when they get it right.' Alex grinned. Although he doesn't say much, he's proud of himself when he does. He handed the phone back to Ellie.

'Or so we tend to think.' Ellie wriggled as she pushed her phone into the pocket of her jeans.

'Am I wrong?' asked Nathan.

James took a sip from his can. 'Well, God shows himself throughout history as a God who is involved with his creation. There are stories from the Bible and stories from people today that tell how God spoke directly to them. Sensible, sceptical, mentally healthy, normal people saw God, heard him, felt him, experienced him so strongly that they had no doubt whatsoever that it was God, and no doubt whatsoever that they must reshape their lives and their futures to do what he told them.'

'If you believe the Bible,' said Ani. 'And that's not the same as coming to earth.'

Jo had returned to her seat. 'Why are we surprised that God should decide to drop in? Nanna enjoys receiving texts, emails, phone calls, even video calls, but they are no substitute for a personal visit. Being with us lets her share our experience of life in a way that no other communication can. Perhaps God felt the same.'

I liked that image.

Alex was apparently less appreciative. 'But Jesus was a fictional character.'

Although I was finding all this to be moving a bit fast for my brain, I thought it was time I showed that I was still in touch and was confident to rebuff this. 'No,' I said, perhaps a little too pompously. 'The historical existence of Jesus has been proven by contemporary documents other than the Bible.'

'So he was a good man. That doesn't make him God.' Nathan took some pretzels from the bowl which Ani offered him, and passed it along. 'You're a good bloke, but God? I don't think so.'

'We could debate that further,' I grinned, pleased to be included.

'Or you could just zap him and prove him wrong, Pete,' suggested Alex.

'If I'm God, I don't need to prove my power.' I lifted my chin to look down my nose at people, but that made me cough, which rather spoilt the impact.

James scratched his head before continuing. 'To Christians, what matters is that Jesus was not just a good man; not just an insightful teacher; not just a clever illusionist: he was God on earth.'

> Later on, the one who is the true Light arrived to shine on everyone coming into the world.
>
> But although he made the world, the world didn't recognise him when he came. Even in his own land and among his own people, the Jews, he was not accepted. Only a few would welcome and receive him. But to all who received him, he gave the right to become children of God. All they needed to do was to trust him to save them. All those who believe this are reborn! — not a physical rebirth resulting from human passion or plan — but from the will of God.
>
> And Christ became a human being and lived here on earth among us and was full of loving forgiveness and truth. And some of us have seen his glory — the glory of the only Son of the heavenly Father! (John 1: 9–14, TLB)
> #

A quick word about the Bible passages. You may find them helpful or distracting. You're the reader. Feel free to read them as you go along or come back to them later.

'Hmmm.' Nathan was sceptical. Frankly, Nathan is always sceptical — not just about God, but about anything that isn't consistent with his thinking. 'We skipped over something here. All this may be very well, *if* you believe in God.' There was silence, which surprised me. I thought someone would leap in. 'What? You're not going to answer that?' I thought someone should, but it was a bit beyond me.

James clearly wasn't troubled by Nathan's challenge. 'Well, we could debate the existence of God for a week, and still not convince the other. I can't prove to you that God exists any more than you can prove to me that God doesn't exist.' He took another unhurried sip from his can. 'What is interesting, though, is that there seems to be a God-created need in the hearts of people throughout history and in most cultures. It seems significant that people on every continent have been trying to connect with God, or some power beyond this earth, since the beginning of time. So it comes down to faith. I choose to believe in God.'

'Why?'

James was thoughtful as he caressed his bearded chin. 'Because it makes more sense to me than believing there is no God. Because believing it makes me a better man and my world a better place. Because Jesus describes a God I want to connect with. And because of my experience of God, influencing my life and my relationship with the world every day. We each believe in something. We each allow our lives to be influenced, even controlled, by something. I choose God.'

'I can relate to that,' said Ellie, 'although I wouldn't have articulated it so well. Thanks James.' James smiled.

Ani frowned. 'That may be very good, but only if you believe the Bible.'

'I think it's the same issue.' James scratched the back of his neck. 'There is abundant evidence that the Bible records events which actually happened, but the Bible interprets those events in a particular way. It assumes that a creator God wants a relationship with his creation, and that humanity wants a relationship with God, and it assumes that God has the keys to how humans can get on with each other. I choose to believe the Bible's interpretation, to believe that it tells how to relate to God and to other people.'

'Hmmm. Maybe we'll come back to that.' Clearly Ani wasn't convinced.

'I have a feeling we will.' Mei smiled as she nodded slowly.

The conversation moved on to other topics as Nathan fired up the barbecue and Ani began to set out salads. Alex sat quietly, until he suddenly said, 'James, you said there were two mysteries. We heard about God coming to earth. So what's the second?'

As always, James was ready with an answer. 'Mystery two is the pregnant virgin.'

Nathan turned from placing meat on the barbecue. 'Ah yes. The pregnant virgin. Fantasy time. It can't happen.'

'I'm surprised that God would risk having people snigger behind their hands by seriously suggesting such a thing?' Ani is almost as sceptical as Nathan. They make a good pair.

> God sent the angel Gabriel to the Galilean village of Nazareth to a virgin engaged to be married to a man descended from David. His name was Joseph, and the virgin's name, Mary. Upon entering, Gabriel greeted her:
>
> 'Good morning! You're beautiful with God's beauty, beautiful inside and out! God be with you.'
>
> She was thoroughly shaken, wondering what was behind a greeting like that. But the angel assured her, 'Mary, you have nothing to fear. God has a surprise for you: You will become pregnant and give birth to a son and call his name Jesus.'
>
> 'He will be great, be called 'Son of the Highest.' The Lord God will give him the throne of his father David; He

> will rule Jacob's house forever — no end, ever, to his kingdom.'
> Mary said to the angel, 'But how? I've never slept with a man.'
> The angel answered, 'The Holy Spirit will come upon you, the power of the Highest hover over you; therefore, the child you bring to birth will be called Holy, Son of God. (Luke 1: 26–35, MSG)

Jo had been quiet until now. 'Well, actually, we now know that a virgin can become pregnant! Reproductive technologies enable women to carry a child without ever having had sexual relations with a man.'

'You're not suggesting that Mary had this technology 2000 years ago.' There was the trace of scorn in Nathan's voice.

'No, but maybe God knew that it was possible.'

'The thing about a mystery is that it can't always be explained — like Ellie's illusionist,' said Mei.

'Isn't that a cop-out?'

I thought Mei was onto something, so I decided to add my bit. 'We humans have convinced ourselves that we're such a clever species that there is nothing we can't know and understand. But there is a simple explanation to the virgin birth.' Everyone looked at me.

'What's that?'

'That God is God!'

'Eh?'

I wasn't sure if they were waiting for me to share a brilliant insight or whether they were waiting for the men in white coats to come. I'd got myself into this. Now I had to get out of it.

'Well, why should we think that God couldn't make a virgin pregnant? If he created the universe and operates it day by day; if he created humankind and all other living things; if he can intervene to change events and to change individuals; then why couldn't he do this simple thing?' There was silence as that thought sank in. They were clearly impressed by my vast intellect. Actually I impressed myself.

'Fair point,' conceded Nathan. 'If you're going to believe in God — if! — there's not much point in putting limits on him.'

'Or her.' Mei smiled broadly.

'Yay Mother God.' Ani laughed and applauded.

Jo looked pensive. 'I'm a Christian, but I'm uncomfortable with the idea of a virgin birth. I think the blokes who wrote the gospels didn't want to suggest that Joseph and Mary could have been up to something.'

That evoked a response, as people agreed or disagreed. I stood and pointed to the barbecue. 'We'll call for a division. Virgin-birthers to the left of the barbecue; non-virgin-birthers to the right.' Surprisingly, nobody moved.

'You're getting caught up in an intellectual debate,' said Ellie. 'Does it really matter? Accept the mystery of it all. James is right. We can't explain everything,'

I thought that was pretty profound. 'That's true. Some people who live healthy lives get cancers; others recover from cancer against all medical explanation.'

'Sometimes the strangest of incompatible couples form long-term relationships.' Ani looked at Ellie and me.

'There are plenty of situations for which there are no explanations, and may never be,' said Ellie.

Nathan looked at James. 'So, James, you're saying that God chose to drop in on planet Earth. He chose to arrive by some miracle.'

'Well, he's God. What else would you expect?'

Mei spoke almost in a whisper. 'Perhaps he still does!'

SOAP OPERA

Sun has set. Barbecued meat and salad. (Sorry vegetarians and vegans. Our group caters for all tastes.)

Ani went into the house to get more food. Nathan checked the progress of the meat and moved some of it around. Some of us clustered at the barbecue. Watching meat sizzle and the fire spit and flare puts me in a contemplative mood.

'Hmmm.' I tried to make my hmmm sound wise and not confused. 'I wonder about Joseph and Mary. Everyone would have assumed they had been … you know. Why would God put them in such an awkward position?'

'Ah,' said James.

'Because God knows us, he knows that we love a soap opera, so the story involves a pregnant teenager and a man prepared to stand by her.'

'It's a familiar enough story,' said Nathan. 'It has happened millions of times, before and since, throughout the world.'

Ellie looked at Nathan. 'Yes, but people's response varies between cultures and over time. What would you have done if you had been in Joseph's situation? His fiancée announces to him that she's pregnant, and he knows the baby is not his. In my understanding of the Jewish community at the time, Joseph would have been within his rights — even within the community's expectations — if he had quietly broken off the engagement.'

'So why didn't he?' Nathan removed meat from the hotplate and placed it on plates.

'God got involved — again,' explained Mei. 'Through an angel and a dream, Joseph was given the message to go ahead with the wedding and accept the child as his own.'

'God told him in a dream?' Ani screwed up her face. 'That sounds like a euphemism for "No one has any idea".'

'It doesn't much matter,' said Ellie, 'because Joseph accepted it. And that says something about Joseph's relationship with God.' I love the way Ellie just cuts through all the discussion to the heart of an issue.

I can do that too. 'Or perhaps he was so in love with Mary that he was prepared to do anything to hold onto her.'

'I didn't realise you were such a romantic, Pete.'

Thank you, Jo. It hadn't occurred to me. Perhaps I am. I found myself smiling unwittingly.

'I imagine that his parents, and perhaps his friends and siblings, would have told him he was crazy, that he should drop Mary because she couldn't be trusted and because his reputation was at risk.' Ani selected a sausage from the plate Nathan had placed on the table. 'People might reasonably assume that the baby was Joseph's if he chose to stay with Mary.'

'But he stayed with her anyway,' said Ellie.

'In the soap opera version, I'd imagine Joseph spending a lot of time standing at a window staring into space with a contemplative look on his face; I see his father and mother yelling at him to reconsider; I see Mary sitting in a chair, weeping alone; and I see gentle moments between Joseph and Mary.' Jo has a fun way of looking at life.

Ani laughed. 'I think you're right. But we would probably quietly applaud him as he stands by her against all critics.'

> *The birth of Jesus took place like this. His mother, Mary, was engaged to be married to Joseph. Before they came to the marriage bed, Joseph discovered she was*

> pregnant. (It was by the Holy Spirit, but he didn't know that.) Joseph, chagrined but noble, determined to take care of things quietly so Mary would not be disgraced.
>
> While he was trying to figure a way out, he had a dream. God's angel spoke in the dream: 'Joseph, son of David, don't hesitate to get married. Mary's pregnancy is Spirit-conceived. God's Holy Spirit has made her pregnant. She will bring a son to birth, and when she does, you, Joseph, will name him Jesus — 'God saves' — because he will save his people from their sins.' This would bring the prophet's embryonic sermon to full term:
>
> 'Watch for this — a virgin will get pregnant and bear a son; They will name him Immanuel (Hebrew for 'God is with us.')'
>
> Then Joseph woke up. He did exactly what God's angel commanded in the dream: He married Mary. But he did not consummate the marriage until she had the baby. He named the baby Jesus. (Matthew 1: 18–25, MSG)

Something else was puzzling me. 'How was Mary chosen from other good Jewish girls who would have been appropriate to carry this baby? Or, come to think of it, how was Joseph chosen?'

'We don't know,' said James. 'But what we do know is that Mary and Joseph both had a strong faith and were open to God's leading. Instead of being fearful, Mary sings a song of praise to God that is full of joy.'

'I think she understood that she had been chosen for a unique role, and she did not take it lightly.' Mei reached for a bowl of pasta salad. 'After the birth of Jesus, when a number of extraordinary things happened, we are told that Mary treasured all these things in her heart and often pondered what they meant.' (Luke 2:19)

'Perhaps she was chosen,' suggested Jo, 'because God knew that she would make an exceptional mother, one who would understand the actions and words of her son.'

'She was not to know that he would strain her patience and understanding as a mother and cause her incredible grief as she watched him being crucified.' Ellie was right about that.

'And we only have glimpses of Mary's reactions to situations she had to deal with,' said Mei. 'Like Jesus teaching the rabbis while still a child; performing miracles; ignoring his mother while he was talking to the crowds; being arrested and tried and crucified …'

'I can't imagine how I would have responded to what Mary had to deal with.' Ellie was sounding quite reflective.

'Which is why you weren't chosen,' suggested Alex.

'That and the fact that you were born 2000 years too late,' Nathan added.

Ellie smiled. 'Nowadays, some branches of the Christian church revere Mary and pray to her.'

I had a sudden memory flash. 'One Roman Catholic friend explained to me, tongue in cheek, that the reason for this is that the best way to get through to a man is to talk to his mother.' This evoked some smiles.

'I think Mary is a worthy role model as a servant of God and as a mother,' said James, 'but the events of Easter and Paul's letters reminds us that the only mediator we have with God is Jesus, and that we need no other — neither Mary nor a priest. We can pray directly to God.'

'Which is pretty fantastic,' Mei added.

POLITICS

Later. On the table are plates containing bones and scraps of uneaten food. While the platters and bowls of salad have been decimated, there are some pickings left, so we're picking.

Stomachs were satisfied, and we were feeling relaxed. 'I thought Mary and Joseph lived in Nazareth. Why did they end up having the baby in Bethlehem?' Ani asked.

'Ah,' said James.

'Because God knows us, he knows we're obsessed with politics, so he orchestrated a census. And typical of all political decisions, its purpose was taxation!'

'Politics? I thought politics was a recent invention.'

I don't think so, Alex. The Greeks invented politics. Or was that democracy? Jo cleared it up before I expressed my ignorance aloud.

'Don't be naïve, Alex. Judea was occupied territory, a remote outpost of the Roman Empire.'

'And was this Emperor Julius Caesar of "et tu Brute?" fame and all that?' asked Nathan.

'Kind of, but a bit earlier. The emperor at this time was Caesar Augustus and he ruled vast areas of the then known world — what we now know as Europe, Asia and North Africa. The empire was held together by large and efficient armies, well equipped, brilliantly organised, and supported by excellent infrastructure such as roads, forts and barracks.' Jo selected a piece of carrot and bit into it.

'Must have been expensive. Armies, weapons …', began Alex, making expansive gestures.

'Tanks, planes, helicopter gun-ships, rockets ….' Nathan grabbed a chop bone and pointed it at him, like a gun.

I grabbed a pair of tongs and pointed them at Nathan. 'Put down the chop and back away.'

'I suggest you cooperate.' Alex tried to sound menacing. 'We have sausages, and this could get ugly.' His ultimatum bought a truce. 'You were saying, Jo?'

Jo shook her head slowly. 'The areas conquered returned benefits to the heart of the Empire — goods like minerals, foods, fabrics, and taxes.'

'So what's with the census?' asked Ani.

Mei took up the story. 'The Emperor wanted to ensure that no-one slipped through the cracks, that every citizen of Rome — and that included everyone in the conquered lands — paid their dues.'

'So they updated their computer records?'

'Don't be silly, Nathan,' I said. 'They probably didn't have reliable wi-fi to connect them with Rome.'

Mei continued calmly. 'The checks were carried out by requiring everyone to travel to the birthplace of their ancestors. If they were married, that meant the birthplace of the husband's father. So Mary and Joseph travelled to Bethlehem.'

'I've heard that the Bible got the politics wrong, that it names the wrong governor or something.' That's a new one on me, Nathan, but I don't feel qualified to correct you.

'You're right,' said Ellie. He is? I thought he was just being his usual sceptical self. 'Luke says that Quirinius was governor of the region at the time, but some evidence suggests that Quirinius wasn't actually governor when the census was taken.' I didn't know that. 'But Luke was recounting the story around eighty years later, so this is an understandable minor error, which I think just adds authenticity to the story.' How do you know all this, Ellie?

> *At that time Emperor Augustus ordered a census to be taken throughout the Roman Empire. When this first*

census took place, Quirinius was the governor of Syria. Everyone, then, went to register himself, each to his own home town.

Joseph went from the town of Nazareth in Galilee to the town of Bethlehem in Judea, the birthplace of King David. Joseph went there because he was a descendant of David. He went to register with Mary, who was promised in marriage to him. She was pregnant, and while they were in Bethlehem, the time came for her to have her baby. She gave birth to her first son, wrapped him in cloths and laid him in a manger — there was no room for them to stay in the inn. (Luke 2: 1–7, GNT)

'I find it interesting that, even before he knew it, Jesus' life was impacted by the realities of politics.' Jo ran her fingers through her blonde curls. 'In his lifetime he had to deal with Roman politics, national politics and religious politics. And all of these came together in his arrest, his trial and his death.'

'God knew the realities of life in our world,' said James.

Mei added, 'He still does.'

ROAD TRIP

Even later. Cake is being passed around. It would be wrong to refuse some.

As the conversation drifted to Christmas plans, it emerged that each of us was planning to go away across new year, so there would be no New Year's Eve get-together. Ellie described our plans. 'We're taking a road trip down the coast, around 1000 kilometres all up. We've often said we'd like to do it, so finally committed.'

'Without kids.'

'Without kids. They'd have been welcome, but they didn't want to come. They're adults with their own lives, so it'll be just us.' She smiled at me.

I blew her a kiss. Then, embarrassed, I decided to fill the pause with noise. 'Which reminds me. I understand that the Romans made Mary and Joseph go to Bethlehem, but why did God make that happen — and so late in the pregnancy?'

'It confirms that God is male,' said Ani.

I ignored that, because I didn't want to be distracted from what I had been rehearsing. 'Well I've been thinking.' There were shocked looks on people's faces, and a number of muttered derogatory comments, which I thought was a bit unkind, but I continued unfazed. 'I've decided that it's simple really.' Now they looked at me with eyebrows raised in expectation.

'Because God knows us, he knows that we love to go on holiday at Christmas, so he included a road trip for Joseph and Mary. And to add further realism, the hotel lost their booking and the maternity hospital was closed for Christmas!'

I looked at James, hoping I hadn't stolen his thunder, but he gave me the thumbs up, while the others applauded.

Alex focused on the practicalities. 'So did they have maternity hospitals in those days?'

I was joking, Alex.

'I think it's highly unlikely,' said James.

'But Because God knows how we love animals, he surrounded the new baby with animals and provided a manger for a cradle.'

He smiled at me and gave another thumbs up. Good follow-up, James.

'Clearly the health and safety people weren't as active in those days,' said Ellie. 'I think we'd be initiating an investigation.' She can't help herself.

Jo grimaced. 'The trip from Nazareth to Bethlehem would have been arduous. It was more than a hundred kilometres on a rough and hilly road. It would have been difficult and may have taken several days. Not something I'd have wanted to do when birth was imminent.'

'Were there no buses or taxis? You know, camels called Hump-free cabs?' I was rather proud of that one.

'No, they had a donkey.' Alex sounded convinced. 'There are lots of Christmas carols that say so. I know my carols.'

'Most of the Christmas carols were composed almost two thousand years later,' said Ellie, 'by people who thought a donkey would be a nice touch to the story. The Bible doesn't say anything about a donkey.'

His face showed his disappointment. '*Little Donkey* won't be quite the same again.'

Mei tried to cheer him up. 'Joseph would have needed transport for his work as a carpenter, so it is probable that Mary would have ridden on the donkey.' Alex looked pleased, as he mimed Mary riding a donkey, although it wasn't very realistic.

'I should hope so! Mary couldn't have walked that far. Believe me, it's bad enough in a car or ambulance.' Ani looked around at the other women, and was affirmed with nods of agreement. 'You men have no idea.'

James, ever the diplomat, moved to quickly smooth the waters. 'You're right, ladies. And we admire the fortitude you show in such situations.'

'Fortitude nothing. Giving birth takes five-titude!' There was a round of applause for Ani from the women.

'Anyway, let's back to the story.' Alex sounded agitated. 'When they arrived, there was no accommodation left. Is that right?'

'Most of us can relate to that.' Nathan stood, put his hands on his back, and rotated his upper body. He has a back problem which is aggravated by sitting for a long time. 'We arrived in Gloucester, England, on the weekend of a football carnival. The only accommodation we could find was a dubious B&B, but it was better than sleeping in the car.'

Ani did not look amused. 'I'm still not sure about that.'

'Mary probably thought that a bed of straw among the animals was preferable to the roadside.' Ellie shivered.

'Some Biblical scholars suggest that Joseph and Mary didn't try to book into an inn. It's more likely that they would have stayed with relatives. Apparently, families often had a guest room at the top of the house.'

I didn't know that, Mei. 'So why the stable?'

'Well, but the house may have already been crowded with visitors in Bethlehem for the census.'

'And the rellies decided the young couple should have the stable? I'm surprised someone didn't give up their bed for Mary.'

It's always seemed wrong to me.

'Perhaps Joseph and Mary arrived late, or perhaps they preferred some privacy for the birth,' suggested Ani.

'My understanding is that the stable was probably a downstairs all-purpose day room, which would also be used to shelter frail animals at night, especially in very cold weather. It would have had troughs for water and hay.' Mei reached forward to cut a slice of cake which she scooped onto her plate.

'Hence the manger,' said Ani.

'So are you saying it is unlikely that Mary and Joseph were surrounded by horses, donkeys, cattle, sheep or goats?' Nathan leaned on the back of a chair.

'Who knows?' James pulled at his beard. 'All the animals in nativity scenes have been added by artists and song writers and story tellers.'

'So even their own donkey SUV — or is a donkey an ATV — was probably parked outside with the other animals, unless the weather was so bad that it was at risk?' I asked.

'Does it matter?' Ellie refocused us. 'The idea that Jesus was born amid animals adds a touch of humanity, of sensitivity, of compassion in us. We love the image of Mary giving birth in such a setting, and then placing her child in a manger.'

'Presumably the animals were all vegetarian, so he was not at risk of being accidentally or intentionally ingested.'

Obviously, Alex. A large cow attacking a baby would be cow-ardly. I didn't say that aloud.

'Mary wrapped him in swaddling clothes, igniting the "To swaddle or not to swaddle" debate.' The others laughed at Jo's suggestion.

'At least he was an easy baby.' Where are you going with this, Nathan? 'The Christmas carol, *Away in a manger*, says "But little Lord Jesus no crying he makes".' There were spontaneous mutterings of 'Yeah, right!' and 'In your dreams!'

'Another fanciful, unrealistic carol.' Ellie waved her hands dismissively.

'That's just kitsch,' said James. 'Jesus would have done what babies throughout all time and all places do.'

I tried to summarise. 'So it's a little unclear why Mary gave birth in such a rough situation and whether animals shared the moment with her.'

'I think so.' James brushed some cake crumbs off his pants. 'But, as Ellie says, does it matter? We sometimes complain that God doesn't understand our issues, doesn't realise what it's like to be human, doesn't understand our difficult circumstances and struggles. The message of Christmas is that he certainly does. Not only did Jesus live as a man, confronted by all the usual difficulties and temptations of humans, he was born on the road away from home. His parents couldn't afford hospital insurance, or even a backpackers' hotel. They got the garage.'

'God knows why,' said Jo.

'But God knows why,' Mei added.

BABY

January 5. Around the barbecue at Jo and Alex's home. Another beautiful summer evening. Dips are being passed around. The barbecue is covered with vegetables, being lovingly supervised by Jo. Apparently, we're 'eating healthy' tonight.

The conversation meandered through Christmas, New Year and holidays. Mei held up her camera to display a photo of a baby.

'We have a new grandchild,' she said excitedly. 'A little girl named Dani. Isn't she beautiful?'

'She is,' agreed Ellie. 'All babies are beautiful, no matter what they look like — if you get my meaning. I just want to hold them.' Ellie was smiling at the thought of it.

'But it's considered weird to ask strangers in the shopping centre if you can hold their baby.' I thought I should remind of community protocols.

'That's true, but, you're right, Ellie. This little one is fascinating.' She put the phone away. 'James hasn't seen her for a week, and I think he's having withdrawal symptoms.'

'Which is why Jesus arrived as a baby.' James did it again — just eased the conversation to matters of faith.

'Eh?' I don't know who said it, but we all thought it.

'Ah,' said James.

'Because God knows us, he knows we can't resist a baby, so that's how Jesus arrived, although a politician, community leader or celebrity — even the child of a celebrity — would have received more media attention.'

'You're right,' agreed Ani. 'Babies are irresistible.'

'But, as James says, look at the options.' Nathan dipped a piece of celery into a dip. I wonder who came up with that name — Dip? It couldn't have taken much intellectual effort. Sorry. Nathan continued. 'God could have arrived on earth in a spectacular display. People would have been awed and terrified. They would have done whatever God demanded. Even the Romans would have been frightened.'

'It would have made more sense if he had come as a religious leader, an influential rabbi?' said Alex. 'He could have changed people's thinking about religion and faith, persuaded them — with human or divine strategies — to change their ways.'

'Or he could have come as a community leader, politician or philanthropist, connected to networks of other influential people who could have financed his cause and introduced him to power brokers,' I suggested.

Alex was waiting to insert another thought. 'I think his best bet would have been to arrive as an actor, singer, professional sportsman or other entertainer. He would have been a media sensation. His Twitter and Facebook accounts would have exploded.' He used his arms to mime and explosion.

I liked that. You win, Alex.

'Even the timing is strange,' said Jo. 'Some spectacular things happened when Jesus was born, and during Jesus' life and after his death, but word about them was spread only by word of mouth and some writings. It wasn't very efficient. Nowadays, Jesus would have live, world-wide coverage; he would have a blog read by millions; he would appear on TV talk shows. Everything he said and did would be uploaded to YouTube, so that it was available to the world.'

'Instead, Jesus came as a baby — dependent, vulnerable, needing to learn everything about himself and his world, striving as he grew to find his place in the world.' Mei smiled. 'Each Christmas we can relate to his very human parents; we can connect with a very human Jesus; we can delight in a very human celebration. And through it, we can be reminded of our own vulnerability and insecurities, and perhaps place our dependence in our heavenly Father. Don't you love God for that?'

'That's all very sweet, Mei, but there's a contradiction here.' We all waited. If there's a contradiction, Nathan will find it. He's more of a lawyer than a vet. 'This vulnerable baby, with poor, blue collar parents, was also a king. *Hark the herald angels sing glory to the new-born king.* And *Noel, noel, born is the king of Israel.* And didn't the wise men come looking for a king?'

I'm surprised Nathan knows more than one carol. I was thinking of several smart retorts, but fortunately James saved me from my own enthusiasm.

'Ah,' said James.

'Because God knows us, he knows we love anything royal. So Jesus was born a King.'

'But his parents weren't royals.'

'He didn't need to go through the stage of prince in waiting, but was born a king. The idea of Jesus being King of kings and Lord of lords means that there is no higher authority. His reign over all things is absolute and unchallenged.'

'How can you be a king if you can't rule over people; and how can you do that if you don't have a base — a palace or castle somewhere?' Good question, Nathan.

'Jesus' kingdom, as he pointed out to his critics, was not an earthly kingdom,' James explained. 'He tried to explain that he seeks to be king over our hearts, our lives.'

'That was a bit difficult for the people of his time to follow,' said Mei, 'and frankly, we sometimes struggle with it too.'

I'm glad Mei struggles with it. I don't feel quite so ignorant.

> *God raised Christ from death and set him on a throne*
> *in deep heaven, in charge of running the universe,*

> everything from galaxies to governments, no name and no power exempt from his rule. And not just for the time being, but forever. He is in charge of it all, has the final word on everything. At the centre of all this, Christ rules the church. The church, you see, is not peripheral to the world; the world is peripheral to the church. The church is Christ's body, in which he speaks and acts, by which he fills everything with his presence. *(Ephesians 1:20-23, MSG)*

'Perhaps it was not about the title, but the assumptions that went with it,' suggested James. 'In Jesus' day — and for centuries beyond — the notion of kingship implied several things that were contrary to Jesus' goals.'

'Such as?'

'Power, for example. Kings expected to be bowed to as they passed. They used violence to hold onto power. They lived lives of comfort and even decadence that is the stuff of fairy tales. They appeared to have no regard for their subjects. But Jesus modelled humility, servanthood, compassion.'

'This was one of the things the disciples didn't understand initially,' said Jo. 'They thought the Messiah would lead them in a battle to evict the Romans.'

'What about inaccessibility, James?' Mei asked. I said they were a team.

James encouraged her. 'Go on.' He ran a finger along an eyebrow.

'Well, you didn't have an audience with the king unless you were powerful and wealthy yourself, a society A-lister. But Jesus was accessible to everyone, even to those considered outcasts. He wanted people to know him.'

'True. Jesus gave us a new type of authority, an expectation that royalty will govern for the good of the people, not themselves.'

'It's a lesson for all leaders,' added Mei. 'Jesus modelled servant leadership, a form of leadership which seeks to uplift others, not themselves. We reject leaders who behave as tyrants.'

Hmmm, I thought. This was all very well, but … So I asked, 'But if he was a king, what's with the shepherds in the Christmas story. They wouldn't have featured on a royal invitation list.'

'Everyone's welcome to meet Jesus,' said Mei.

SHEPHERDS

Later. Empty plates are scattered on the table.

The barbecued vegetables were very tasty. We continued to pick at the few pieces remaining on the platters.

Then Ellie said, 'Pete has a point.' I do? Maybe we're a team like James and Mei. 'A king is born — and the first people to be told about the birth were shepherds.'

'The media must have been furious,' Alex waved his hands in emphasis. 'They should be the first to be told about everything — according to them.'

'Not the media; not the town mayor; not the priest; not the tax office; not even the local infant health nurse. Shepherds!' I lifted my hands for effect too.

'Are you having a dig at farmers?' Ani pressed her lips together. 'I come from farming stock …' Then, as she realised what she had said, added … 'so to speak.' We laughed.

'Those from farming stock often farm stock,' said Nathan.

'And stock farms,' laughed Alex.

I explained. 'I assure you that no criticism nor offence to today's sheep farmers is intended, nor should it be inferred. They were different blokes in a different place in a different time.' Then I turned to James. 'So why the shepherds?'

'Ah,' said James.

'Because God knows men, he knew that blokes would relate to shepherds — men who slept in the open, wrestled wild animals, ate meat and didn't bathe for weeks on end.'

Jo beamed. 'And because he knows women, he knew that they wouldn't need to be patronised.' She and Ani laughed, and high-fived one another.

'This is the story of a baby,' said Ani. 'I would have expected women to be first on the scene? But no — men! How very traditional.'

'To be fair, Jo,' Mei responded, 'theirs was a very masculine society. Women ran the household and raised the children. Men held all the important roles in the community and were expected to provide for their families.'

'Sure, but the shepherds were not gentlemen, men of learning, men of enterprise, men of status or men of influence. These were workers, probably looked down on when they walked the streets or entered the temple, perhaps somewhat scruffy and on the nose.'

I quickly interjected. 'Again, farmers, please do not take offence. He's speculating about a time before hot showers.'

'Shepherds.' Mei shook her head. 'We joke, but it's almost unfathomable.'

'Almost,' said James. 'But the shepherd is a powerful image in the Bible, a metaphor for God's great care for us.'

> *Like a shepherd, he [God] will care for his flock, gathering the lambs in his arms, hugging them as he carries them, leading the nursing ewes to good pasture. (Isaiah 40: 11, MSG)*

> *The LORD is my shepherd, I lack nothing. He makes me lie down in green pastures, he leads me beside quiet waters, he refreshes my soul. He guides me along the*

> right paths for his name's sake. Even though I walk through the darkest valley, I will fear no evil, for you are with me; your rod and your staff, they comfort me. You prepare a table before me in the presence of my enemies. You anoint my head with oil; my cup overflows. Surely your goodness and love will follow me all the days of my life, and I will dwell in the house of the LORD forever. (Psalm 23, NIV)

'There aren't many places in the world where the traditional, nomadic shepherd, persists, are there?' Ellie looked around the group.

Nathan answered. 'Actually a lot more than you might think. But even in places where modern technology and modern farming methods have taken over the farm; where the shepherd may have thousands of sheep, use vehicles to monitor them and fences to contain them; he or she still cares for them, assists with lambing, hand feeds the lambs if necessary, provides water and food during times of drought, rescues them from floods, uses vaccinations and other measures to ensure their health. Isn't that right, Ani?'

'Absolutely. While the cynic will recognise that the sheep are an investment to be protected, those who live in rural areas know that farmers also have an attachment to their sheep, caring for them for reasons which have nothing to do with economics.'

'Shepherds play a role in several of Jesus' parables,' said Mei. 'And Jesus even described himself as the Good Shepherd, who cares for the sheep; protects them against predators or thieves; searches for those that wander off; and leads them to good pasture and water. His sheep know his voice and he knows them.'

> I am the Good Shepherd. The Good Shepherd puts the sheep before himself, sacrifices himself if necessary. A

> hired man is not a real shepherd. The sheep mean nothing to him. He sees a wolf come and runs for it, leaving the sheep to be ravaged and scattered by the wolf. He's only in it for the money. The sheep don't matter to him.
>
> I am the Good Shepherd. I know my own sheep and my own sheep know me. In the same way, the Father knows me and I know the Father. I put the sheep before myself, sacrificing myself if necessary. You need to know that I have other sheep in addition to those in this pen. I need to gather and bring them, too. They'll also recognise my voice. Then it will be one flock, one Shepherd. (John 10: 11–16, MSG)

James added, 'He even used the image to explain that he wasn't just interested in the Jewish people. God cares for all people. Jesus came to live and die for all people. The offer of a fulfilling life following Jesus is for all people.'

'So let's not knock the lowly shepherds. Is that the point?' I thought a summation was called for.

Ellie was reflective. 'Well, we are often guilty of measuring a person's status not so much by the importance of what they produce or do, but by their wealth and visibility. But Jesus always supported and loved those who were considered outcasts in his community.'

'He still does,' said Mei.

CONCERT

A bit later still. Alex found some meat, and claimed it was near its 'use by', so decided to cook it. Since he went to the trouble, I guess I'd better have some, right?

Alex emerged from the house carrying a plate of meat and placed it next to the barbecue.

Jo watched him, but didn't leave her seat. 'What is it about men and meat?' she asked.

Alex reignited the flame under the hotplate. 'It's James' fault.' James looked surprised, and scratched the top of his head. 'It was the talk of shepherds and his description of them that made me want meat.' I'm not sure he convinced anyone, but it obviously sparked a thought in Ellie.

'We talked about why God chose shepherds to be the first to hear the news of Jesus' birth,' Ellie said, 'but we didn't mention the way the news was spread — singing angels! Why not a notice in the local paper?'

'Ah,' said James.

'Because God knows that we love an outdoor concert, he had the message delivered by an angel, backed by a full choir, with their own lighting and sound system. A bit over the top perhaps, but why should God do things by halves?'

'And they had no mobile coverage in the paddock, so they couldn't access their social media accounts.' Good one, Alex.

I tried to imagine it. 'A massive light shone from the sky. It must have been like the arrival of an alien space ship in a sci-fi movie.'

Nathan had wandered over to the barbecue and was watching Alex's cooking technique. 'Have you noticed that despite all the imagined high brain power and technological prowess of aliens, they can't see in the dark, because their vehicles always arrive at night and have blindingly bright lights?'

'But the shepherds hadn't seen alien movies, so they wouldn't have assumed an alien invasion.'

Well, it's logical, isn't it? Jo thought so.

'And as the shepherds were reaching for their sunnies, an angel appeared to announce the news that the promised Messiah, the "Christ", had been born. I like that the angel's first words were, "Don't be afraid!" Very sensible.'

'The lead singer is joined by a choir, a backing group extraordinaire, all singing a cappella,' explained Mei. 'And then they were gone.'

'What happened to peace and goodwill to all men?' Alex turned the meat. 'And hopefully a little to women as well.'

James had decided to check out the barbecue too, and stood with the other two. 'What they sang is often translated as peace and goodwill to all humankind, but is better translated as peace to those with whom he is pleased or to those who honour him.' He stabbed a sausage with his fork and dropped it onto a plate.

'If the news had been announced to the Mayor, he would probably have asked his secretary to put a visit in his digital diary for next week or whenever he could fit it in,' said Ani.

'And if the news had been given to priest, he might have felt the need to point out that they were not members of his church,' Jo suggested.

Ellie added, 'And if God had organised a press release, the media would have focused on the health and safety issues associated with the stable.' Well it is her job.

'Whatever the reason for God making his announcement to shepherds,' said Mei, 'they responded and went looking for Jesus. Perhaps that was the key to their role.'

'I can't imagine the shepherds keeping the news to themselves.' Ellie shook her head to Alex's offer of a chop. 'I wonder who else they told.'

Alex placed a plate of meat on the table, and settled into a chair. 'If I was their boss, I'd have wanted an explanation for why they left the sheep in the care of an apprentice and a work experience student. And I doubt I would have been convinced by stories of angel choirs and the like.'

'Nor would their mates.' Nathan was taking time to choose a piece of steak.

'Or a wife?' I queried.

'I suggest you don't try it,' said my beloved. I smiled at her sheepishly. (Sheepishly. Did you get that?)

> There were some shepherds in that part of the country who were spending the night in the fields, taking care of their flocks. An angel of the Lord appeared to them, and the glory of the Lord shone over them. They were terribly afraid, but the angel said to them, 'Don't be afraid! I am here with good news for you, which will bring great joy to all the people. This very day in David's town your Saviour was born — Christ the Lord! And this is what will prove it to you: you will find a baby wrapped in cloths and lying in a manger.'
>
> Suddenly a great army of heaven's angels appeared with the angel, singing praises to God:
>
> 'Glory to God in the highest heaven, and peace on earth to those with whom he is pleased!'
>
> When the angels went away from them back into heaven, the shepherds said to one another, 'Let's go to Bethlehem and see this thing that has happened, which the Lord has told us.'
>
> So they hurried off and found Mary and Joseph and saw the baby lying in the manger. When the shepherds

> saw him, they told them what the angel had said about the child. All who heard it were amazed at what the shepherds said. Mary remembered all these things and thought deeply about them. The shepherds went back, singing praises to God for all they had heard and seen; it had been just as the angel had told them. (Luke 2:8-20, GNT)

'You said, James, that the shepherds were there to appeal to the men.' Alex managed to get his question out while chewing vigorously. 'The angels were probably there to appeal to the ladies.'

'I don't see why.' Jo shrugged her shoulders. 'I think most of the angels in the Bible were men.'

I hadn't thought of that.

Apparently nor had Alex. 'Then why is it always the girls who dress as angels in nativity plays?'

'That's probably because the boys all take the roles of wise men and shepherds.' Ani's explanation seemed logical.

There was a pause in the conversation, before Jo said, 'What bugs me is that I see Jesus as a man's man, yet he is often depicted quite differently by artists and song-writers.'

A man's man. I'd never really thought about that.

'Perhaps it's because Jesus was caring, a man who spoke with children and had compassion for those who suffered — qualities that are more typically associated with women,' said Ellie.

'Perhaps. But this was a man who single-handedly overturned the tables of people who were trading money and sacrifices in the temple, then, grabbing a whip from someone, he drove the traders out of the temple. He stood up to the powerful religious leaders of his time and called them hypocrites. When faced with a crowd who were ready to throw him off a cliff, he stared them down and walked through them. He went to Jerusalem knowing that the religious leaders were out to kill him, and despite the warnings of his friends.' Jo was clearly moved by what she said. And she was right.

I decided to add my knowledge. 'And when given the opportunity by the Roman governor to speak in his own defence, he refused, and even antagonised the man with the power to condemn him. Instead, he endured whipping, beating, torture, and cruel crucifixion, along with public humiliation and scorn.'

'And on top of all this, this was a man who had something worthwhile to say, whose words challenged, taught, guided, encouraged and inspired,' added Mei.

'And he repeatedly stood up for women in a society where women had limited power,' added Ellie.

'That's an interesting point, Ellie,' said Jo. 'The gospel of Luke, in particular, recounts a number of stories about women, or which might have particular appeal to women. Some of these he alone records.'

'Like what?' asked Nathan.

Clearly, this issue was important to Jo. 'Well, for example, he records the events around Mary's pregnancy, including her visit to her also-pregnant cousin, and her song of joy. Luke tells about a woman in a funeral procession weeping for the loss of her son. Jesus feels compassion towards her and brings the boy back to life.'

'I wonder if that ruined the reputation of the funeral director.' My comment was ignored.

Jo continued. 'In another story, Jesus defends a prostitute, who bathes his feet with tears and perfume and weeps for his forgiveness. And I love the story of the day Jesus visits the home of two of his friends, Mary and Martha, and is caught up in an altercation between them, because one does all the work preparing lunch while the other simply sits and listens to Jesus.' Jo smiled. 'Women of any generation and culture can relate.'

'Frankly, so can men,' contributed Nathan. 'Some men are like blisters: they don't show until the work is done!'

'Only Luke,' said Mei, 'tells how Jesus uses the image of a woman who loses a coin, and searches the house until she finds it, as an illustration of how God searches for "lost" people. And he recounts the story of the "prodigal son", who wastes his inheritance, but is welcomed back by his father with love and celebration. And only Luke tells the story of the "good Samaritan", who helps a Jew who has been attacked and robbed, while those who would be expected to help him avoid him.'

'You lot are on a roll.' Nathan was about to eat the last morsel on his plate. 'I'm impressed by your knowledge and your passion.'

Mei smiled. 'We all know about the twelve closest friends or disciples who travelled with Jesus, but Luke points out that there were women disciples too. He even lists their names.'

'Really? Who were they?' I didn't know about women disciples. Was that even legal?

'Sorry, Pete, you'll have to read Luke to find out.' Sneaky.

'Women were important to Jesus and to the story of his life and death.' Jo tilted her head. 'I like the fact that they were there from the beginning, are there at the cross watching him die, and were the first to know of his resurrection.'

'This is all very interesting, but I thought the Christian church was all about men, with women being kept in their place.' This seemed to be an issue for Ani, and she's not entirely wrong.

'Unfortunately,' said James, 'there's some historical truth in that — even some contemporary truth — but Jesus was one of history's great liberators of women.'

'And still is,' said Mei.

WISE MEN

Quite late. Coffee and cake. Have I room?

As we collected coffee and cake, some of us sat down again in different seats. I made coffee for Ellie and settled into the chair next to her.

'Can I back-track a bit?' she asked.

'In the absence of a chairperson, ladies and gentlemen, shall we put the matter to a vote?' I asked.

She ignored my interruption, with practised ease. 'We questioned why God chose humble shepherds to hear the news of Jesus' birth first. But what about the wise men. They weren't exactly blue-collar.'

'Ah,' said James.

'Because God knows us, he knows we can't get enough of celebrities, so he sent men who were important enough to get an audience with King Herod. And because God knew they would be keen on cross-promotion with other celebrities on social media, he sent a star for them to "follow".'

We all smiled at his pun. I wish I'd thought of that. 'So who were these wise men?' I asked. 'No-one invited me.' Their smiles became more like smirks.

James rubbed the side of his nose. 'The "wise men", as they are commonly called, visited Jesus because they understood him to be a king. They were Magi, astronomers and astrologers from somewhere east of Judea. They saw signs in the stars that indicated the birth of a king — not just an ordinary king, but a very great king, which is why they made a journey to visit him.'

'And they came a fair distance,' Mei added.

'How do you know that?' asked Ani.

'Well we assume they set out on their journey when Jesus was born. They made the mistake of visiting Herod to ask where they could find the child. It made sense. They were looking for a prince, and Herod was the king, so they would have assumed that the baby was born into Herod's family.'

'And they must have been impressive,' said Ellie. 'Probably wealthy, wise, exotic. Impressive enough to turn up at Herod's door and get to see him.'

James took a sip from his coffee. 'Although he hid the fact, Herod was alarmed by their story. He was cruelly jealous of his power, and wasn't about to allow the emergence of a pretender to the throne. He asked them when the star had appeared, to work out approximately when Jesus had been born, then murdered all boys up to the age of two, to ensure that this potential threat was eliminated. That suggests that when the Magi arrived in Judea, Jesus was approaching two years old. So we assume this journey had taken close to two years.'

'But nativity scenes are usually displayed with shepherds and wise men visiting Mary, Joseph and Jesus in the stable, with Jesus still a baby.' Alex was right, of course.

Mei joined in. 'As we've observed before, artists and song-writers add their own touches. The family wouldn't have still been living in a stable more than a year after the birth, although they were apparently still in Bethlehem.'

'How do we know there were three of them?' Alex held up three fingers, in case we didn't know how many three were.

'We don't,' said Ellie. 'We just assume there were three because they brought three gifts — gold, frankincense and myrrh — but that is conjecture. We don't actually know how many there were.'

'And I reckon they would have had a large entourage,' said Jo. 'A trip of more than a year's duration across desert country would have required ongoing resources — bedding, food, equipment, and servants to attend to it and to the Magi.'

'I suppose the Magi add a touch of wealth, status, colour and pageantry compared to the shepherds. Perhaps this was to appeal to the wealthy, who can't relate to shepherds.' Mei broke off a piece of cake and put it in her mouth.

'As always, no offence to shepherds is intended nor should be inferred,' I quickly added.

> Jesus was born in the town of Bethlehem in Judea, during the time when Herod was king. Soon afterward, some men who studied the stars came from the East to Jerusalem and asked, 'Where is the baby born to be the king of the Jews? We saw his star when it came up in the east, and we have come to worship him.
>
> When King Herod heard about this, he was very upset, and so was everyone else in Jerusalem. He called together all the chief priests and the teachers of the Law and asked them, 'Where will the Messiah be born?'
>
> 'In the town of Bethlehem in Judea,' they answered. 'For this is what the prophet wrote: "Bethlehem in the land of Judah, you are by no means the least of the leading cities of Judah; for from you will come a leader who will guide my people Israel."'
>
> So Herod called the visitors from the East to a secret meeting and found out from them the exact time the star had appeared. Then he sent them to Bethlehem with these instructions: 'Go and make a careful search for the child; and when you find him, let me know, so that I too may go and worship him.'
>
> And so they left, and on their way they saw the same star they had seen in the East. When they saw it, how

> happy they were, what joy was theirs! It went ahead of them until it stopped over the place where the child was. They went into the house, and when they saw the child with his mother Mary, they knelt down and worshipped him. They brought out their gifts of gold, frankincense, and myrrh, and presented them to him.
>
> Then they returned to their country by another road, since God had warned them in a dream not to go back to Herod. (Matthew 2:1-12, GNT)

'On a different matter, why are we so fascinated by celebrities? There are millions of people across the globe who spend hours every week following what their favourite — or least favourite — celebrities are doing and saying. They may be sports-people, entertainers or 'socialites' — people who perform no useful role except to be seen and photographed — yet they are accepted as authorities on all sorts of topics. To many people, the political, social or religious views of their favourite celebrity must be 'right', even though the person may have no greater knowledge or insight into the issue than anyone else.' There was a bit of passion in Nathan's voice.

Ani apparently felt the same way. 'I agree, Nathan. We also over-use the word "star". Why are people with a high public profile, especially in the world of entertainment, called stars?'

I decided it was time to shine. 'I think it's fitting, because a star is a speck of light that looks attractive, but is so far away it is completely inaccessible and not bright enough to light our way effectively.' That brought a couple of nods.

'Perhaps the reason we call them stars is that we see them as people to follow, as the Magi did so long ago. It is kind of sad that we see celebrities as heroes. It is a false concept. A celebrity has nothing to offer except their fame; a hero is famous because of what they have already given.' That's good, Jo; very pithy.

'I think we spend too much time following the wrong people,' said James. 'The star that the Magi followed shaped their pathway. The stars we follow shape ours.'

'That's true,' said Ani. 'We all have role models, people we follow: parents, friends, famous or not-so-famous people who have made a mark on the world and on us. We watch them — how they live, what they say, what they do.'

Mei made me wonder when she commented, 'Interestingly, we all have someone who watches *us*! I'm not referring to stalkers, but to ordinary people who follow what we love, what we say, what we do. There's a good chance we don't know it, but we are influencing someone.'

Hmmm. It made me wonder who I influence. It's a bit of a worry.

'The Magi were changed by a cosmic event. Perhaps their visit to Jesus was also a cosmic experience, which changed them and those they knew for the remainder of their lives,' said James.

'It certainly changed me,' said Mei.

SANTA

Late. Empty plates. No room for more food. Although chocolate isn't really food is it?

'There is something — or someone — we have overlooked in our recent discussions; someone very important that we haven't mentioned.' We all looked at Ellie expectantly, trying to think who she meant. 'Santa!' Her face lit up. 'Where does Santa Claus come in?'

Santa! I didn't think of that, Ellie.

'Ah,' said James.

'Because God knows us, he knows we love a good celebration, so he knew that Jesus' birth would result in a wonderful birthday party every year. And because he knows how kids love presents, he gave us Santa Claus.'

Ani laughed. 'We do like to party. I love getting together with you lot to share stories, tell jokes, laugh, sing, dance, with good food and drink at the centre of it. I think it's universal.'

Probably so, but I've yet to see much dancing, Ani.

'A birth, a birthday and Christmas are three of the most popular occasions for a party, and all three are represented at Christmas!' Jo stood and danced a little. 'Party time!'

Nathan dampened her enthusiasm. 'What's with the nativity plays? And worse, adults dressing as characters from the nativity. I think that's ridiculous.'

'Oh, lighten up, Nathan,' said Jo. 'Some of us enjoy theme parties.'

'People dress as their alter-ego — far too many wise men or angels; too few shepherds; and we are always interested to note those who see themselves as the stars of any show and appear as Mary or Joseph!'

'I like dressing as a wise man, with fancy robes and the trappings of wealth and wisdom,' I said.

'Exactly.' I guess I walked into that one.

'Well I think the Christmas story is amazing, and I love it.' Ellie wasn't about to be subdued. 'Every year, I put our nativity set on display, and re-read the story from the Bible.'

'When our kids were little, we told the story to them as we took it out of the box.' I enjoyed that ritual with our kids.

'You don't have to believe the story of Christmas to enjoy Christmas,' said Nathan.

'That's true of course, which is where Santa comes in.' Mei handed him a chocolate, which he began to unwrap.

'James, you claimed that God gave us Santa.' Ani took the chocolate from him, and Mei handed him another. 'Really?'

'Well, you know, of course, that the name is a distortion of "Saint Nicholas".' James wiped the corner of his eye. 'In the fourth century, Nicholas was a bishop in Myra — now in Turkey. His parents left him a fortune when they died, but he was a kind and generous man who gave money to the poor, often secretly. He was later made a saint for his good works. Over the centuries, a practice evolved of giving secret gifts at Christmas, and these were attributed to Saint Nicholas. But by the sixteenth century, Saint Nicholas was losing favour to "Father Christmas" as someone who gave presents to children at Christmas. His image as a rotund elf who dressed in red and rode a sleigh pulled by reindeer was built on a range of stories, perhaps the most significant of which was *A visit from Saint Nicholas* ...'

I know that. ''Twas the night before Christmas, when all through the house, not a creature was stirring, not even a mouse ...'

I was interrupted by Ellie. 'Thank you, Pete. We'd rather hear James.' Bit harsh, I thought. I like that poem.

James beamed. 'Such praise! I'm all overcome.'

'You'll get over it.' There was a touch of sarcasm in Mei's tone.

He did, contentedly chewing on the chocolate he had just put into his mouth.

'I did an internet search one day and there were so many stories about Saint Nicholas, it was hard to distinguish between fact and myth.' Alex's gesticulations were inhibited by his efforts to unwrap a chocolate.

'I agree,' said James. 'But what matters is that Saint Nicholas was given a compassionate heart by God. He is a model for Christian living, teaching us to show both compassion and practical assistance to poor and struggling people — hopefully, not just at Christmas!'

I liked James' idea that God gave us Santa. I hadn't thought of it that way.

Mei looked at Nathan. 'Nathan, you said that anyone can enjoy Christmas, even if they don't believe the Christmas story. The problem with that is that Christmas has taken on a variety of meanings. Ask people what Christmas means and you will get a number of cynical answers such as stress, expense, over-eating, getting drunk and visiting in-laws!'

'True, but beyond the cynicism, you hear answers like a time for family.'

'Or a time for friends.' Ani made a sweeping gesture to include us all.

'A time to bury the hatchet and to forgive,' said Nathan.

'Or to turn a blind eye to things. We may have been speeding, but fair go, officer — it's Christmas!' Alex illustrated his story with gestures.

'A time to give gifts,' said Ellie. 'And, of course, a time for holidays.'

'A time of peace.' Alex held up his hand in the V peace sign. 'Peace and goodwill.'

'These are all wonderful meanings for Christmas,' said James, 'but they are not the real meaning of Christmas. At Christmas we celebrate the birth of Jesus, when God became a human and lived among us. As Christ, the promised Messiah, he came to save us from ourselves, to show us how to develop a relationship with God so that we can really live life to the full!'

'What does that mean?' Alex spread his arms. 'My life's pretty full.'

'Don't confuse a life that's full with a life that's fulfilled. Our diaries can be full, but our lives empty. Don't assume that the pain and regrets of the past have to be part of your future. God offers possibility and hope. Don't assume that the clutter of your life is immovably rusted in place. God can clean out the shed. That's fulfillment.'

Mei said, 'Long before Saint Nicholas, God played Santa. He gave us the gift of Jesus.'

'The gift that keeps on giving.' Ellie hesitated. 'This is a gift for all humanity forever, for all people in all times and all places. He is the gift who connects us with God, who enables us to be friends with God.'

> Yes, God will give you much so that you can give away much, and when we take your gifts to those who need them they will break out into thanksgiving and praise to God for your help. So two good things happen as a result of your gifts — those in need are helped, and they overflow with thanks to God. Those you help will be glad not only because of your generous gifts to themselves and to others, but they will praise God for this proof that your deeds are as good as your doctrine. And they will pray for you with deep fervour and feeling because of the wonderful grace of God shown through you.
>
> Thank God for his Son — his Gift too wonderful for words. (2 Corinthians 9: 11–15, TLB)

'The problem is,' said Mei, 'that it's easy to allow the many meanings of Christmas, the clamour and the commotion, to crowd out the real meaning. God walked among us. He still does.'

SEQUEL

Later than late. More coffee? No? I think Jo wants to go to bed. I think perhaps we all should.

'So that's the end of the Christmas story.' Ellie stifled a yawn. 'Sorry. That was interesting — and it made me think. What shall we talk about next?'

'Ah,' said James.

'Because God knows us, he knew we'd like prequels and sequels. Long before Star Wars confused us with a succession of prequels, God had written a prequel and two sequels to the Christmas story. Without the sequels, the story doesn't make much sense.'

'Really?' asked Ellie. 'What's the prequel?'

'Hundreds of years before the birth of Jesus, a prophet predicted that all this would happen. His name was Isaiah, and he spoke of a day in the future when a child would be born.'

> *For to us a child is born, to us a son is given, and the government will be on his shoulders. And he will be called Wonderful Counsellor, Mighty God, Everlasting Father, Prince of Peace. Of the greatness of his government and peace there will be no end. He will reign on David's throne and over his kingdom, establishing and upholding it with justice and righteousness from that time on and forever. The zeal of the LORD Almighty will accomplish this. (Isaiah 9: 6–7, NIV)*

'This was interpreted by the Jewish people as the Messiah, the one who would save them from successive invaders. So when Jesus arrived, performing miracles and teaching people about God in a way they had never heard before, they assumed him to be the Messiah or the "Christ". The disciples didn't see it for a while. They just thought he was an impressive teacher. But then, when Jesus finally asked them outright, Peter got it: He announced, "You are the Messiah, the Son of the living God."' (Matthew 16: 16, GNT)

'Well that was good, wasn't it?' asked Alex.

'Certainly. But the problem was that Peter and the other disciples misunderstood what Jesus would do as Messiah. They assumed, right up until Jesus' death, that he would call down angels or inspire the fighting men of the land to overthrow the Romans. They struggled to understand that Jesus wasn't interested in such things.'

'And why not?'

'Well it's obvious.' Nathan stretched. 'You can never defeat violence and the threat of violence. In war, there are no winners, just those who dominate for a time. You may repel one army from your borders, but another will follow.'

'That's right, Nathan,' said Mei. 'Jesus came to bring peace — not just peace between opposing armies or gangs, but triple peace.'

'Triple peace?' It was unusual for Alex to be so engaged.

'Peace between God and us,' said James. 'We don't have to fear God's alienation if we mess up. We are at peace with him. At Christmas, God offered to humankind his peace and his goodwill, his best wishes if you like. He still does.'

Jo covered a yawn. 'Sorry. It's past my bedtime.' Then she added, 'I like to think that God greets us like we would greet a much-loved friend that we haven't seen for some time. He greets us with enthusiasm and a huge smile on his face. He puts his arms around us and says "I'm so glad to be with you. I love the peace between us."'

'Peace within us,' added James. 'Many people talk of peace, but are torn by poor self-image, depression, defeatism, a lack of acceptance of themselves. They struggle to change. But when we know that we are loved by the creator of the universe; that he loves us unconditionally no matter what our past or future; that there is nothing we have to do to earn his love; that he will always, always, always, love us; that's a game changer.'

'When you put it that way,' said Ellie, 'how can we not find peace within us?'

James continued. 'And peace between us. Jesus pointed out that anyone can show love to people they care about. He urged us to love our enemies, and to say a blessing on the people who curse us. This was new teaching which would change the world.'

'And still does,' added Ellie.

Nathan stood up. 'I love the peace between us, too, but I fear that if we don't go home, that peace might be stretched.'

'You're probably right.' Alex stood too, and reached for Jo's hand to help her up. 'James, you said there is a sequel to the story of Christmas.'

'That's right. Without the sequel, the story doesn't really make sense. But I think we should explore that another night.'

'And it's better than Christmas,' said Mei.

BECAUSE GOD WANTS A RELATIONSHIP WITH US ... WE MEET HIM IN PERSON, NOT JUST ONLINE

Christmas is a celebration of the birth of Jesus. Who was Jesus? Where does he fit into the God picture? And if he is God, why would he want to spend time among humans, with all our self-centred obsessions?

The fundamental message of Christianity is that God is accessible. This is unbelievable — almost. Why would the Creator of the universe want to connect with humanity? If the amazing and tragic and exciting and bewildering story of Jesus is somehow connected to God, what was God thinking?

It's simple really.

The reason God gave us Jesus is that God wants a relationship with us.

Let me show you.

MEETING

February 16: Our home. A really hot night after a forty-degree day. There are many legs and arms on display. We're enjoying drinks, but no-one wants to eat yet. We have the table set up next to the barbecue, so we are seated in a circle on comfortable outdoor chairs.

We shared stories about holidays and family and work and kids and ... you get the idea. Then Alex surprised everyone by saying, 'You messed up my holiday, James. You made me think, and I don't like doing that on my holidays.'

'Or any other time,' I suggested.

James was a little more gracious. He always is. I wish I was like that. 'I'm sorry, Alex. How did I make you think?'

'When we were together last, we talked about Christmas, and you said that Christmas has a sequel? Do you remember that?'

'I do. In fact, two sequels. Without them, Christmas is just a party: stressful lead-up, short-term fun, but nothing more. When it's over, there's just an empty feeling, a bin full of torn gift wrap, a stack of empty bottles and a fridge full of leftovers; nothing more, nothing lasting.'

'Well now we're here, are you going to tell us about the sequels?'

'The first sequel is that God wants a relationship with us.'

'How do you know that?'

'Ah,' said James.

'Because God wants a relationship with us, he thinks about us and he knows that we think about him — although we're sometimes shy about admitting it. So he moved on from messaging and arranged to meet.'

'I must have been away that day,' said Alex. 'When did this happen?'

'Through Jesus. God has always met with people — in visions, in dreams, in voices, through prophets, through miracles … lots of ways. He has messaged us repeatedly. But for most people, it was a bit like meeting online, lacking the personal touch. There's nothing like meeting face to face.'

'You're right,' said Ani. 'In my online business, and especially through my blog, I try to be as relational as possible. I even connect to some customers by phone. But I sometimes wish I could talk to them face to face.'

James pulled his right ear lobe. 'Remember the truth of Christmas? God came to earth as a human. And when we meet Jesus, we meet God.'

'Why would God want to do this?' Nathan leaned back in his chair, stretched his legs and took a sip from his can.

'Because God wants a relationship with us — a real and authentic relationship.'

'Hang on,' said Ani. 'Back up. God thinks about us?'

'I believe that.' Jo brushed something from her T-shirt. 'We are his creation, so I'm sure he thinks about us, worries about us, wants the best for us. He can see us heading for trouble and tries to warn us.'

Ellie nodded agreement. 'Sometimes he physically intervenes, but not always, because we often prefer to learn from our own experience, and because he didn't create us to be puppets and toys. But when we mess up, he is there to pick up the pieces, to help, to offer guidance, to assure us of his forgiveness and to teach us how to forgive ourselves.'

'Why would God care? He's boss of the world. He can make us do whatever he wants.' Ani isn't easily persuaded, but I respect that.

'He is our Father, and this is the way a parent would fee,' said Jo. 'We didn't decide to call him Father to get a share of the inheritance. Jesus told us to do it. Throughout the gospels, Jesus repeatedly referred to God as his Father and ours. He even taught us to pray to God as Father.'

'And he knows we think about him at least some of the time,' added James, scratching his cheek.

'If you're a Christian, maybe, but not me,' said Nathan.

James smiled. 'It doesn't matter whether we are Christian or of some other faith or a declared atheist — we often think about God. Whenever our emotions catch us off guard, by-passing our conscious thought, we call to him.'

Ellie was having difficulty opening a can because of her long fingernails. She passed it to me. 'That's true. There is an endless list of emotions which evoke a spontaneous outburst of "Oh my God", "Jesus", "Thank God", "Christ", or something similar. We do it when things are good and when things are bad; when we are at peace or panicking; when we are overflowing with joy or drowning in despair; when we are feeling tenderness or anger … There are lots of circumstances in which we call out God's name.'

'Many people tell of a time when they made a deal with God,' said Jo. 'Finding themselves in a seemingly irretrievable situation, they promised God that if he saves them, they will change their lives in some way, serve him in some way.'

There was a moment's silence. Nathan balanced the can on one knee. 'But when I say "Oh my God" or similar, it's just an unthinking outburst. I'm not really calling to God. And when people are desperate, they're just clutching at straws.'

'Perhaps,' said Mei, 'there's something sub-conscious happening. As James and Ellie noted, it doesn't matter if our cry to God is unconscious, or if we think of it as a form of abuse, God is in our thoughts. It's because he put himself there, ensuring we are constantly reminded that he is there — here — ready and willing for us to grow our relationship with him.'

'So this God I haven't met wants a relationship with me, and thinks I want a relationship with him, because I yell his name when a drop a hammer on my toe?' Nathan's tone was almost sarcastic.

'Think about your relationship with Ani.'

Ani reached over and held his hand. 'Yes, do that.'

'You may not want to admit it, but she's on your mind constantly. When you're shopping, you see something she would like and you think of her. You see an ad for a movie, and you think "Ani would enjoy that". You are at work and you suddenly think, "I wonder what Ani's doing right now?" You're driving home and you are picturing your evening together.'

He paused. Everyone was looking at Nathan, whose brow was furrowed. Ani broke the silence. 'I think of you like that.'

Nathan said, 'Well of course you're right, James, but what's that got to do with God?'

Mei jumped in. 'I think James is saying that, in the same way as our minds drift subconsciously to the people we love, they also drift to God. He has planted himself in our thoughts too.'

Nathan was looking uncertain. 'So is God just a stalker?'

'In a way,' said James, 'but a good way. He really wants a relationship with us, and he will keep pursuing us until we catch him.'

I smiled instinctively. 'That was a tricky switch. Until we catch him, not he catches us.'

James smiled. 'God will never compel us, never force us. He waits lovingly for us to respond. Just as Jesus did. Jesus showed love, compassion, care for people in a way they had never seen before, and he invited them to follow him. Many responded to his love.'

'And millions still do,' said Mei.

> *Long ago God spoke in many different ways to our fathers through the prophets, in visions, dreams, and even face to face, telling them little by little about his plans.*
>
> *But now in these days he has spoken to us through his Son to whom he has given everything and through whom he made the world and everything there is.*

God's Son shines out with God's glory, and all that God's Son is and does marks him as God. He regulates the universe by the mighty power of his command. He is the one who died to cleanse us and clear our record of all sin, and then sat down in highest honour beside the great God of heaven. (Hebrews 1: 1–3, TLB)

BOUNDARIES

Night. Plates are laden with salads, onions and meat.

I lit the barbecue and cooked onions and a variety of meat, while Ellie arranged plates of salads. Several of the group helped with the preparations. Some were standing with me at the barbecue. There's something very social about standing around a barbecue with friends.

'You said, James, that God has always told people who he is and what he expects. So why decide to send Jesus?' Fair question, Ellie.

'Ah,' said James.

'Because God wants a relationship with us, he wanted to make the boundaries clear. Although we don't read instructions, he knows we are obsessed with "How to do it" clips on YouTube. So he said, "Here's Jesus. Watch and learn!"'

I love the way James does that — puts it in a contemporary setting. Although I wasn't saying much — cooking needed my attention — I was listening, and I asked, 'What do you mean by boundaries?'

'The early books of the Old Testament are filled with laws, details about how to live in a way that honours God and enables people to get along together and stay healthy. We think of these as God pointing his finger and saying sternly: "Do it or else!" But it's probably better to think of them as boundaries that enable us to have a right relationship with God and sound relationships with other people — and even a proper perspective on ourselves.'

That makes sense. That's what laws are always about really — setting the boundaries.

Mei elaborated. 'Jesus reminded us that all these laws really amount to two things: Love God, with your heart and mind and body; and love other people unconditionally. That's what it all comes down to. They're the boundaries.'

'Easier said than done.' Alex spoke quietly, but we all heard.

'Exactly.' Jo nodded at Alex. 'So God sent us Jesus to be our model and example, to show us a new way of relating to God and a new way of relating to one another.'

'So suddenly God decides to be kind, instead of vengeful.' Nathan's eyebrows expressed disbelief.

'God has always been kind.' Jo unexpectedly giggled as she swallowed a mouthful of food. 'That's better. The notion of a loving God was not new. It's not like God suddenly changed his character. There are many references in the Bible before Jesus that tell of God's love and care and compassion and faithfulness.'

'Absolutely.' James pulled at some of his moustache hair. 'But through Jesus, God highlights certain aspects of his character.'

'Like what?' asked Alex.

'He is holy — perfect and good. He thinks of us as his children. He forgives us when we do wrong. He'll do whatever it takes to connect with us. We should stop nit-picking the laws, and looking for loopholes. Instead, follow the spirit of the laws. Or, better still, watch Jesus and see how he behaves. Do you want me to keep going?'

'No, I think I get that.'

'Well, because we're sometimes a bit thick when it comes to understanding these things, Jesus gave practical meaning to his teaching by telling parables — stories with a deeper meaning. While we might shut down if we think we're being lectured to, we are seduced by a story, so parables are a subtle way of getting a point across.'

'I think of a parable as a story that keeps on giving,' said Mei. 'People living in a different time and place can read the story and interpret it in their context.'

'So Jesus preached lots of sermons and told lots of stories. Do as I say.'

I admire Nathan's persistence. And frankly, he makes me think about things I've never given much thought to. Perhaps that's why I don't have the confidence to answer — or ask — questions like Ellie does. I'm glad God gave me Ellie. God gave me Ellie? Why did I say that? I thought I gave me Ellie.

'Anyway,' said Ellie, 'Jesus wasn't all talk. The Bible says a lot more about what Jesus did than what he said. He modelled — he lived — the behaviour he wanted us to follow. Not just do as I say, but do as I do. For example, he talked with, even touched, outcasts; he dined with collaborators; he healed the child of a Roman soldier — ostensibly the enemy; he helped people with disabilities; he treated women, even a prostitute, with respect and compassion; he gave time to children; he showed humility, even when people wanted to make him into a celebrity.'

> Jesus resumed talking to the people, but now tenderly. 'The Father has given me all these things to do and say. This is a unique Father-Son operation, coming out of Father and Son intimacies and knowledge. No one knows the Son the way the Father does, nor the Father the way the Son does. But I'm not keeping it to myself; I'm ready to go over it line by line with anyone willing to listen.
>
> 'Are you tired? Worn out? Burned out on religion? Come to me. Get away with me and you'll recover your life. I'll show you how to take a real rest. Walk with me and work with me — watch how I do it. Learn the unforced rhythms of grace. I won't lay anything heavy or ill-fitting on you. Keep company with me and you'll learn to live freely and lightly.' (Matthew 11: 27–30)

'Jesus' life still stands as an example of how to live. He took God's boundaries and showed how they applied to our lives every day.' Jo cut a piece of chicken.

'Is that the "What would Jesus do" thing?' asked Ani.

'Yes,' said James. 'His behaviour so strongly showed God's values that Christians faced with moral dilemmas often try to imagine how Jesus would respond to the situation. Some even wear a WWJD bracelet to remind them.'

'Even without a bracelet, Christians still do,' said Mei.

MOVING IN

Later. Fruit pie for dessert. With ice cream and cream, of course.

We were suddenly surprised by two additions to the group. Our 20-year-old daughter, Gabby, arrived with her friend, Arun. They greeted Ellie and me, then the others, introducing Arun to those he had not met.

'Come and join us,' said Ellie. 'There's not much food left, but you're welcome to what's here.'

Arun noticed a couple of chairs against the wall and inserted them into the circle of chairs.

Gabby was well known to our friends, who questioned her about her studies, her work, her life. 'I've moved back in here with Mum and Dad.' She gave a beaming smile to Ellie. 'I was missing them.'

Ellie smiled back. 'And we were missing her.'

'And wanted to keep an eye on what she was up to.' I laughed.

'And help me,' added Gabby. 'Sometimes it's good to have parents around. I moved in last week.'

'Just like Jesus,' said James.

'Eh?' I can't believe how deftly James segues into talking about God.

'Ah,' said James.

'Because God wants a relationship with us, he moved in, lived with us.'

'To keep an eye on us?' I asked.

'Perhaps,' said James. 'But not to criticise — more to help, to show us how to make decisions, how to live a healthy, fulfilled life. Like you and Ellie do for Gabby. Right?'

Ellie was first to respond. 'Absolutely. There's not point simply criticising. Gabby's old enough to make her own judgements.'

'And probably wouldn't listen anyhow,' I added. I passed some pie to Gabby and Arun.

'And are you saying we're like that?' asked Jo. 'God moved in because we don't really listen?'

'I think that's a good way to look at it,' said Mei. 'Jesus gave us articulate, insightful words. He gave us miracles that attracted our attention. But God knows we need more than clever words and magic tricks. So he gave us an authentically human Jesus, a man who lived as we lived, felt the emotions we felt, dealt with the stresses we experience, and was tempted by things we can relate to.'

'What would have tempted Jesus?' asked Alex.

'This pie.' Gabby laughed, as she tried to wipe cream from her chin. 'It's delicious.' Arun grabbed a table napkin and wiped her chin for her. Aw. That was sweet. I caught Ellie's eye and she winked at me.

James explained: 'The Bible says that Jesus was tempted to use his Godly powers for selfish purposes, for his comfort and survival. At the time, he was in the desert alone, and had been for forty days. He was hungry, thirsty, uncomfortable. If we found ourselves with "magic" powers in such a situation, would we use them for our own comfort? Almost certainly. But Jesus refused.'

'But he survived anyway.' Alex shrugged. 'Perhaps he knew he would.'

'Perhaps,' agreed James, scratching his forehead. 'He was also tempted to play games with God's protection, to leap from a high cliff and let the angels save him. They would have, of course. With similar powers would we have been tempted to jump out of a plane without a parachute — to chase the ultimate thrills, knowing that God would protect us? Highly likely. But Jesus refused.'

'But it would have been a buzz.' Alex made a fist, which he shook quickly, to emphasise his excitement at the thought.

James continued: 'He was tempted to use his power to take over the world, to assume control of the palace, with its status and influence and wealth, to live a life of luxury, with his every need attended by servants.

Would we use such powers for our own gain, to achieve wealth and status and fame? Probably. But Jesus refused.'

Ani deposited an empty plate on the ground beside her chair. 'So what's your point.'

'I get it,' said Jo. 'The point is that Jesus experienced the same sorts of things that matter to us. Read the gospels. Jesus was a real man, touching and touched by the world in which he lived.'

'But he must have been a bit above it all, wasn't he?' asked Nathan.

Mei shook her head gently. 'Not at all. He had a group of close friends, with whom he travelled and lived for three years. This enabled him to explain things to them at a depth that he couldn't explain to other people; to show a vulnerability he couldn't show to others; to express a depth of feeling he couldn't express to others.'

'But no women.' Gabby raised her eyebrows, so it was probably more of a question than a statement.

'Actually, there were women in his life too,' said Mei. 'We talked about that one night. There were female disciples, and even very close friends like Mary Magdalene and sisters Mary and Martha. There's no indication that he had any romantic attachments, despite what novelists and screenwriters might imply, yet, as a man, he must have experienced such feelings.'

'So everyone loved him.' As usual, Nathan was persistent. 'That made it easy for him.'

'To the contrary,' said Ellie. 'He was under constant pressure to please — to lead a fight against the Romans, to perform miracles, to tell great stories. Instead, he criticised the powerful religious leaders; socialised with Roman collaborators; talked to and even touched lepers and outcasts; and gave time and respect to women.'

Mei added, 'Jesus experienced the pressure to be popular, to be liked, but his focus was truth, not popularity.'

'He always drew a crowd to hear him and see his miracles.' I thought I should add my knowledge. 'He probably had his own groupies or fan club.'

'Probably so. We know that he had lots of disciples in addition to his intimate twelve, because at one time he sent seventy out into the villages to spread his message. Some were secret followers, watching and listening from the sidelines. Others would have been observers, entertained by his activities, or by his interaction with the religious leaders, and anticipating the trouble which was to come. Perhaps there were even journalists, or their equivalent, recording the key events.'

'But he knew how fickle people can be,' said James. 'He knew they could turn at any time. Even one of his closest friends, Judas Iscariot, betrayed him.'

> *What shall I say about this nation? These people are like children playing, who say to their little friends, 'We played wedding and you weren't happy, so we played funeral but you weren't sad.' For John the Baptist doesn't even drink wine and often goes without food, and you say, 'He's crazy.' And I, the Messiah, eat and drink, and you complain that I am 'a glutton and a drinking man, and hang around with the worst sort of sinners!' But brilliant men like you can justify your every inconsistency! (Matthew 11: 16–19, TLB)*

In my mind, I recalled the lead up to the events of Easter. 'A crowd welcomed Jesus into Jerusalem as a king, cheering him and creating a pathway of coats and palms — their version of a tickertape parade. Yet only days later, that same crowd, prompted by agitators planted by the religious leaders, called for Jesus to be crucified.'

'Quite true.' Jo paused. 'Given what happened at Easter, we have to acknowledge that he experienced pain — even fear.'

'Absolutely.' Mei looked at the ground. 'As a human, he knew that his death would be painful and degrading, so he prayed to his Father, questioning whether this was really necessary, yet committing to going through with it.'

'And knowing that soldiers were likely to come for him at any time, he asked his closest friends to keep an eye out for him. What did they do? They fell asleep. Three times he urged them to watch his back while he prayed; three times they fell asleep.' Ellie shook her head. 'Yet he didn't berate them. He simply reminded them that it is easy to fall asleep when we should be wide awake, to miss seeing things we should be watching out for.'

'And he wasn't just talking about soldiers, but all the temptations and troubles we face in life,' said James.

I decided it was time for me to lighten the conversation. 'Jesus also understood about being hungry. When Jesus stopped to speak to crowds of people, word spread rapidly, even without Twitter. People came from nearby towns and homes and factories and office towers to listen to him. These weren't planned meetings to which everyone was urged to bring a picnic tea and a gold coin donation, so they grew hungry as the day wore on. So Jesus fed them — 5000 men plus women and children, who didn't get counted in those days; and on another occasion about 4000 men — ditto the comment about women and children, dogs, donkeys and other accoutrements. Fish burgers appeared to be a crowd favourite, because he provided one of the meals from bread and fish.' I smiled smugly.

What, no applause? Don't you people have a sense of humour? Ellie smiled.

Then Ani asked, 'Did Jesus have a family?'

'Of course,' said James. 'We know he had siblings. One brother, my namesake, became a leader in the early church. Jesus understood that family members sometimes want us to live their way rather than our way, to fulfil their needs and hopes rather than following what we believe to be our calling. On one occasion, someone brought word to him that his mother and brothers were waiting to speak to him, but he refused to stop what he was doing to go to them.'

Nathan laughed. 'I wonder what was said later over dinner!'

'I love how Jesus, dying on the cross, asked his friend John to care for his Mum like his own mum and asked his Mum to care for John like her own son.' Ellie spoke very quietly.

'That's beautiful.' Gabby reached for Ellie's hand and held it.

'Look, we could go on all evening talking about Jesus' humanity,' said Mei. 'He caught fish and provided food. He experienced grief and compassion and sympathy. He recognised suffering and pain and injustice, and got upset about abuse of power and privilege. He told stories about sheep, sowing grain, weeds in the crop, muggers on the road, cooking, fishing, lost money, being picked on by bullies, being woken in the middle of the night, young people who want to live the high life, and parents who love their kids no matter what. He helped people who were physically and mentally ill. He attended weddings; experienced the death of a friend; saw the lengths that people would go to in order to help a friend.'

'So your point, Mei?'

'That Jesus was as human as any of us. But he was also God.'

'Which is where this discussion started,' said James. 'Because God wants a relationship with us, he moved in, lived with us. Read the gospels in the Bible — Jesus' story told by Matthew, Mark, Luke and John — and you will meet Jesus, a real person, a man who understood our humanity because he was one of us, who understood our life because he lived it.'

'And still does,' said Mei.

RELATIONSHIPS

Getting late. Coffee — from our new coffee machine.

We had heard little from Gabby and Arun during our conversation about faith, but their faces showed they had been listening intently. As I made a coffee, Gabby commented: 'This all seems a bit heavy for a barbecue. Are your barbecues always like this?'

'Not always. Sometimes they're heavier!' Ellie laughed. 'Lately, we've talked a bit about faith, with some interesting perspectives from James and Mei.'

'This business about God moving in with us.' We all looked at Arun. 'Nice way to put it, but Jesus must have found pretty quickly that we humans are not very good at relationships. I mean we get on fine with friends and people who are encouraging and affirming, but many relationships become competitive or abusive if people don't get their own way.'

That's true.

'Ah,' said James.

'Because God wants a relationship with us, he wants us to have a better relationship with one another, so he blew our minds with a stack of new ideas about relationships.'

'What new ideas?' Arun was getting into the spirit of it.

'If we want a relationship with God, we need to love people too, and not just our friends or those who think like we do. God takes it a step further — actually a giant leap further: he expects us to love everyone.'

'A bit unreasonable, don't you think?' Nathan fiddled unsuccessfully with the coffee machine. I went to help him.

'I agree,' said Ani. 'You're saying we have to love the boring uncle, the neighbour with the motorbike, the drug dealer who hangs around the local shops, the vandal who painted graffiti on our wall.'

James took a sip of his coffee, which he was obviously enjoying. 'I'm not saying it. God is.'

Their body language suggested that Ani and Nathan were finding this a difficult concept.

Mei took up the point. 'Let's clarify this. God is not saying that these behaviours are acceptable — especially not the boring uncle who corners us every Christmas! He's not saying we should condone the drug dealing. Or that we can't ask the motorbike owner to buy a functional muffler. We're not asked to turn a blind eye to divisive or criminal or even unkind behaviour. The example which Jesus gave us is to care about people, no matter who they are, what they do, how far up our noses they get, how much we abhor their actions. We care. That's what love is. Just look out for them, try to help them, show them that they matter.'

Ellie saw that I was doing no better with the coffee machine than Nathan, so showed us how — which didn't inhibit her ability to follow the conversation. 'Jesus didn't just hint that we should try to like these people a little bit more, to be a little bit more patient, a little bit more understanding, a little bit more compassionate. He turned accepted values on their heads to change the way people think about relationships.'

'I don't know that he changed mine.' Alex shrugged one shoulder.

'Actually, he did,' said Jo. 'It's just that you grew up in a society based on his way of thinking, so you weren't aware of it.'

'What do you mean?'

'Well, Jesus summarised it as doing for other people what you want them to do for you.'

'I thought that was: Do to others before they do it to you.' I gave one of my broad smiles. 'Only joking,' I added quickly.

Mei suggested a more authentic way to interpret it. 'One translation of the Bible says, "Ask yourself what you want people to do for you, then grab the initiative and do it for them."' (Matthew 7:12, The Message)

> You have heard that it was said, 'An eye for an eye, and a tooth for a tooth.' But now I tell you: do not take revenge on someone who wrongs you. If anyone slaps you on the right cheek, let him slap your left cheek too. And if someone takes you to court to sue you for your shirt, let him have your coat as well. And if one of the occupation troops forces you to carry his pack one mile, carry it two miles.
>
> You have heard that it was said, 'Love your friends, hate your enemies.' But now I tell you: love your enemies and pray for those who persecute you, so that you may become the children of your Father in heaven. For he makes his sun to shine on bad and good people alike, and gives rain to those who do good and to those who do evil. Why should God reward you if you love only the people who love you? Even the tax collectors do that! And if you speak only to your friends, have you done anything out of the ordinary? Even the pagans do that! You must be perfect — just as your Father in heaven is perfect. (Matthew 5: 43–48, GNT)

With Ellie's intervention, Nathan had finally obtained a coffee and returned to his chair. 'The best thing about loving your enemies is that it gets right up their nose. They don't know how to respond.' That brought a laugh.

'That's actually very insightful. When we change the way we treat people, we change them — not just enemies; anyone.' Jo ran her hand through her short hair. 'As a teacher, how I treat students has a big effect on how they see themselves and how they behave or perform.'

'Jesus pointed out that what goes on in our hearts affects what we do. Get your thoughts right and your behaviour will be all right too.'

That's what I was just thinking, Mei.

James ran his hand around the back of his neck. 'Jesus surprised people by putting a new slant on their laws. For example, if you want God to forgive you, make sure you forgive others. Do good to people who hate you. Bless people who curse you. You know not to murder, but don't even be angry with people. And you know not to commit adultery, but don't even look at a woman lustfully.'

'Except your wife.' I received a punch from Ellie.

'There was more, of course, but I think the point is made. These ways of thinking were not just novel, but downright radical to Jesus' listeners. It went against what they were used to seeing in their religious leaders or hearing from them. What's more, they were impressed that Jesus spoke of these things with authority, like he knew what he was talking about.' James paused, and stared into his coffee. 'Imagine a world where everyone followed such teachings.'

'Just imagine,' murmured Mei.

SEQUEL 2

Late. Don't you people have homes to go to?

I decided it was time to wrap up the evening. Despite the coffee, I was tired. 'Well folk. As much as I enjoy your company, I think it's time Ellie and I went home.' There were some quizzical looks. 'Oh, that's right, we are home.'

Ellie shook her head, and muttered, 'That's not polite.'

Mei laughed. 'No, he's right, Ellie. We should let you get to bed, and get ourselves to bed too.'

'Before you go.' What now, Alex? Did I not make my point clearly enough? Apparently not, because Alex continued: 'I remember you telling us, some time ago, about sequels to the Christmas story, James. Do you remember?'

'Of course, and I've only told you one sequel — that because Jesus wanted a relationship with us, he moved in.'

'So what's the other sequel?'

'Christmas sequel number two is the Easter story.'

'Easter? What about Easter?'

'Ah,' said James.

'Because God loves us, Easter is more than a heart emoji.'

'What do you mean by that?'

'In our modern world, we throw around the word love willy-nilly. People message a hundred friends with "Love you guys" and attach heart emojis to their messages, even to people they hardly know. God's love is neither superficial nor insincere.'

'More than an emoji, oh, so much more,' said Mei, quietly.

BECAUSE GOD LOVES US ... EASTER IS MORE THAN A HEART EMOJI

Like Christmas, Easter has become a secular celebration, with fancy hats, rabbits, Easter eggs, hot cross buns, and even Easter presents. It's Christmas all over again, with variations.

But people throughout the world understand the religious significance of Easter. Many worship in churches at Easter if at no other time of the year. They ascribe meaning to crosses and other Easter symbols.

Easter celebrates the death of Jesus on a day we call 'Good Friday'. How could this Jesus, a man who showed love for the unloved in the community, and tried to teach a new way for humans to relate to one another, be the target of a campaign so vicious it resulted in his torture and death? What was God thinking?

It's simple really. The joy of Easter is that it shows that God loves us.

Let me show you.

LIMB

April 20: Easter. Jo and Alex's home again. Weather is a little chilly, but the company is warm. Assorted appetisers are on hand.

Obviously, the conversation drifted to Easter. It was Ani who started it.

'I'm confused about Easter. I thought Easter was a sad time, but it's a happy time, although I don't really understand the focus — hot cross buns, eggs, school hat parades, and, of course, the shops encouraging us to give presents. What's it all about?'

'Ah,' said James.

'Because God loves us, he wanted us to love him back. Being there when we needed him didn't convince us, and nor did messages relayed by his friends. So he went out on a limb for us — on a particular kind of tree.'

'By the "tree" you mean the cross, don't you?' asked Ellie. 'He hung on it, held by nails in his hands and feet. Death was drawn out and painful.'

I think we get that, but when it's put bluntly like that, well, it makes you think.

'And just to make sure we were noticing, it was preceded by an unjust arrest, a mock trial, abuse and torture.'

> So Pilate took Jesus and had him whipped. The soldiers, having braided a crown from thorns, set it on his head, threw a purple robe over him, and approached him with, 'Hail, King of the Jews!' Then they greeted him with slaps in the face.
>
> Pilate went back out again and said to them, 'I present him to you, but I want you to know that I do not

find him guilty of any crime.' Just then Jesus came out wearing the thorn crown and purple robe.

Pilate announced, 'Here he is: the Man.'

When the high priests and police saw him, they shouted in a frenzy, 'Crucify! Crucify!'

Pilate told them, 'You take him. You crucify him. I find nothing wrong with him.'

The Jews answered, 'We have a law, and by that law he must die because he claimed to be the Son of God.'

When Pilate heard this, he became even more scared. He went back into the palace and said to Jesus, 'Where did you come from?'

Jesus gave no answer.

Pilate said, 'You won't talk? Don't you know that I have the authority to pardon you, and the authority to — crucify you?'

Jesus said, 'You haven't a shred of authority over me except what has been given you from heaven. That's why the one who betrayed me to you has committed a far greater fault.'

At this, Pilate tried his best to pardon him, but the Jews shouted him down: 'If you pardon this man, you're no friend of Caesar's. Anyone setting himself up as 'king' defies Caesar.'

When Pilate heard those words, he led Jesus outside. He sat down at the judgment seat in the area designated Stone Court (in Hebrew, Gabbatha). It was the preparation day for Passover. The hour was noon. Pilate said to the Jews, 'Here is your king.'

They shouted back, 'Kill him! Kill him! Crucify him!'

> Pilate said, 'I am to crucify your king?'
>
> The high priests answered, 'We have no king except Caesar.'
>
> Pilate caved in to their demand. He turned him over to be crucified.
>
> They took Jesus away. Carrying his cross, Jesus went out to the place called Skull Hill (the name in Hebrew is Golgotha), where they crucified him, and with him two others, one on each side, Jesus in the middle. (John 19: 1–19, MSG)

'Why all the drama?' Nathan swallowed whatever he had been chewing. 'The people of the time were familiar with unjust use of power and cruel punishments. The Romans had lined an entire road with crucifixions of Jews who tried to overthrow them. Blood sports involving humans were a popular form of entertainment for the Romans. You said earlier that Herod murdered all babies under the age of two — at least, all the boys — in order to eliminate the threat of a pretender to the throne.'

'Yes, but Jesus had no aspirations to overthrow any government or invader. This was a man of peace, a teacher, whose goal was not to assume earthly power, but to refocus people's attention on God.' Jo shivered as she pulled a jacket from the back of her chair, and dragged it around her shoulders.

'But events took on a momentum of their own, didn't they?' said Ellie. 'When Jesus left the countryside and entered Jerusalem he was received by a great crowd of enthusiastic supporters, which alarmed the religious leaders. They wanted him discredited and dead before his growing support did their credibility any more harm. Pontius Pilate, the Roman governor, tried to appease the Jewish leaders by having Jesus whipped, assuming that this would suffice, but when tensions began to threaten the peace of this outpost of the Empire, and therefore his own reputation and career, he washed his hands of the whole affair, and authorised Jesus' crucifixion.'

'Politics at his birth; politics at his death.'

'Well said.' Thank you, Ellie, but I didn't even realise I had spoken aloud. Everyone looked at me like I had made a profound utterance.

Nathan refocused our attention on James. 'You said Jesus went out on a limb — good pun, by the way — but it wasn't his choice.'

'Well actually, it was.' James scratched the back of his head vigorously. 'Jesus knew he was going to die. The Bible recounts a moving scene shortly before Jesus is arrested. It's night and he is in a garden, praying. He asks his friends to stay awake and keep an eye out for trouble, but they keep falling asleep. Jesus pours out his heart to his Father. He knows what's coming. He agonises over the impending pain and degradation which he knows will come. "Please," he says, "does it have to be this way?" He prays with such passion, is in such physical and mental agony, that he sweats blood. Yet, each time he feels overwhelmed, he says that he is willing to go through with it if that's God will.'

It went very quiet, as we each pictured the scene. Speaking gently, Mei added, 'Things could have been different. He prevented his friends from fighting off the soldiers who came to arrest him. He refused to defend himself when the Roman governor invited him to do so. He allowed himself to be mocked and killed. He allowed himself to suffer, to be crucified, to be the ultimate sacrifice.'

'So that's why lots of people and churches have statues or paintings of Jesus on the cross.' Ani's statement was really a question.

'Right, but I like the cross without Jesus on it — like this.' Jo held up a small gold cross hanging around her neck.

'The empty cross,' said Mei. 'Many people forget that the real focus of Easter is not Jesus' death, but his resurrection.'

James nodded. 'Absolutely. If the story ended at the cross then it would simply be the tale of a religious fanatic who naively misread the power of religious politics. Christianity would have disappeared as a small sect within the Jewish faith. Instead all of this was just the forerunner to the most momentous issue — Jesus' resurrection!'

Nathan frowned. 'Really? Could it really have happened?'

'Humanly, of course not,' said James, 'but Jesus' power wasn't human. What we know is that, apart from the empty tomb, the empty grave clothes, and the messages of angels, Jesus was seen alive on several occasions by a total of more than 500 people.'

'But is all that credible?' Clearly Nathan was not convinced. 'The Roman authorities suggested it was just a story put about by his followers.'

'True, but the facts say something different.'

'OK. Convince me.' Nathan leaned forward.

'Let me.' Go for it, Ellie. 'There were Christ's own predictions — that he would rise again after three days. Towards the end of his ministry he took great pains to prepare his disciples for what would happen — his suffering, rejection and his resurrection. If this hadn't happened, he'd have been labelled as insane or self-deceived.'

'Fair enough. What else?'

'Jesus was seen by numerous people on several occasions. They are recorded by each of the gospel writers and Paul, I think.' Ellie looked to James for support.

James responded. 'Spot on, Ellie. You could start with John 20 and 21, and 1 Corinthians 15. At the time when this was recorded in writing, the authors point out that most of those people were still alive, so were able to confirm or refute the story.'

'But the disciples could have got together and concocted the story.'

Ellie resumed her defence. 'Of course, but if the gospel writers had fabricated the story, you would think they would have got their stories straight. They didn't. There are minor discrepancies between the various reporters, who each observe, recall and focus on different aspects of the story. However, the reporters agree on the key events: the tomb was empty when people visited it; Jesus appeared in person to the disciples and others on several occasions; Christ had risen.'

'Maybe he wasn't actually dead.' It was like watching a tennis match.

'His side was pierced with a sword. He was wrapped in grave-clothes and covered in spices. A massive stone was placed across the entrance to the tomb. Roman soldiers guarded the entrance, in case Jesus' followers tried to steal the body.'

'Sounds pretty dead to me.' I didn't mean to be flippant, but it does, doesn't it?

'Someone could have made up the story and others just believed it because they wanted to.'

'Of course, but look what happened afterwards. Millions of people, probably billions, have lived and died for this story.'

James gently pulled at his short beard. 'I agree, Ellie. Perhaps the most significant evidence of the resurrection is the activities of the disciples in the years following the resurrection. They spread throughout the known world, telling about Jesus' life, death and resurrection. Several of them were cruelly tortured and killed because they refused to recant their story. Many people will live a lie, but only the deranged would suffer horrible tortures and death while stubbornly persisting with a lie.'

'For two millennia,' said Mei, 'the Christian Church has impacted history throughout the world. The Church is founded on the belief in the resurrection. If Christ did not die, then this history rests upon a deception. Paul put it bluntly, "If Christ was not raised, then our gospel is null and void, and so is your faith." (1 Corinthians 15: 14 NIV).

Ani looked around the group. 'You're all very convincing.'

Jo shifted the focus. 'All this is very interesting, but it's not about being convinced with logic. The bottom line is that faith is faith. Faith starts where science and logic and proof run out. There are lots of ways people have tried to explain away the resurrection, but we all believe what we choose to believe, and I'm more convinced that Jesus rose than that he didn't. That's where Christian faith starts. Faith is being certain of the things we can't actually prove, and convinced that the things we hope for will actually happen. And I'm certain, not because of logical argument, but because of my personal experience.'

'Wow. Me too,' said Mei.

LITIGATION

Later. Sizzling barbecue. The aroma of meat hanging in the cold air with the smoke.

After a short pause as Alex and Jo placed bowls of food on the table, lit the barbecue and began cooking, Ani resumed our conversation about Easter.

'What I don't get is why Jesus died in the first place. Clearly God could have prevented Jesus' suffering, so why did he allow this?'

It was a fair question.

'Ah,' said James.

'Because God loves us, he wanted us to know we are forgiven for the things we do wrong. But we are obsessed with litigation and compensation. So he handed over Jesus to take the punishment in our place. Now, in God's eyes, the penalty is paid and we are pardoned. Sack the legal team and move on.'

'What punishments?' Ani was getting into this.

Mei offered an explanation. 'Just like our laws, the Jewish religious laws had an associated penalty for law-breakers which involved a sacrifice. Depending on the severity, offenders were required to kill anything from a small bird to a bull as an offering to God — and sometimes to cook it so that God would smell the aroma.'

'Would God really have been chuffed about the smell of burnt pigeon interrupting his Sabbath afternoon?' I asked. I didn't get an answer, but I wasn't really expecting one.

'Unfortunately,' Mei continued, 'the people had become so obsessed with the sacrifices that an industry had grown up around the provision of animals. Jesus' death replaced the sacrifices. Forget about sacrifices, Jesus is saying, because you're more concerned about getting them right than getting your behaviour right. I will be the ultimate sacrifice to cover every sin. Now, focus on doing what is right, not on the fine you need to pay for each sin.'

I thought that made sense. So did Alex. 'That figures. Stop focusing on the penalty, and focus on avoiding the sin in the first place.'

'So how does that work then?' asked Ani. 'I've never been much into sacrificing animals.'

Alex spoke from the barbecue. 'There are a few animals here that have sacrificed for you.'

'The difference is that they don't realise it.'

'Exactly, Pete. Whereas Jesus did.' James nodded pensively. 'How it works, Ani, is that we admit our sin to God; ask his forgiveness; then change our ways. That's why Jesus died. Sin has consequences, but because of God's ultimate forgiveness, we can draw a line under it and start again.'

'Christians are always talking about sin,' said Nathan. 'What's sin?'

James answered. 'Sin is simply something we do which is contrary to God's law and offends him.'

Ani looked at Nathan. 'Anytime you're ready, I can point out some of your sins that offend me.'

Ellie smiled. 'Believe me, I know how you feel.' What did she mean by that? 'But that's not what God would say. He would say, "I forgive you."'

Ani looked at Nathan. 'OK. I forgive you.'

'Forgive and forget?' Don't push it, Nathan.

'Just be happy with forgive, eh?' Then, turning to Mei, she asked, 'And that's what God says, is it? I find that difficult to believe. I thought God punished people if they did wrong.'

I was surprised at the way Ani was persisting with this.

'Jesus' death and resurrection introduced a new deal, a new agreement, a new testament. He says, "I don't hold your past failings against you."'

'Really? I feel like I've got bad history with God. I wasn't always the angelic person you see before you now.' Nathan didn't appear troubled, but Ani quickly added. 'It's OK. Nathan knows everything. He's forgiven me.'

'And I love you, my Precious.' Nathan took her hand.

'If Nathan can forgive you and love you no matter what, don't you think God can do the same?' asked Mei. 'After all, God is love.'

> *This is how much God loved the world: He gave his Son, his one and only Son. And this is why: so that no one need be destroyed; by believing in him, anyone can have a whole and lasting life. God didn't go to all the trouble of sending his Son merely to point an accusing finger, telling the world how bad it was. He came to help, to put the world right again. (John 3: 16–17, MSG)*

> *And God showed his love for us by sending his only Son into the world, so that we might have life through him. This is what love is: it is not that we have loved God, but that he loved us and sent his Son to be the means by which our sins are forgiven. (1 John 4: 9–10, MSG)*

'Well, you've messed with my head.' Nathan stood at the barbecue, selecting meat and placing it on two plates. 'This doesn't work. God is capricious and cruel, causing pain and death at a whim, through earthquakes and plane crashes and wars and all manner of violence. Where's the forgiveness? And anyway, some of the people who die are supposedly good Christian people.'

'You ask a question that's been asked since the beginning of time,' said James.

'Then how come we don't know the answer yet.'

'Perhaps we humans aren't as smart as we think. The Bible explores this theme. The book of Proverbs is full of wise advice which we still quote to this day. The writer implies that if you do the right things, you will live a happy life. The writer of Ecclesiastes questions this, pointing out that good men sometimes suffer and bad men sometimes prosper. The book of Job then picks up the theme with a long, imaginary story. In it, Job suffers terribly, even though he is a good man who serves God. His friends make long speeches pointing out that Job must have done something very wrong to be punished this way, although Job argues his innocence. Despite all that is said and done to Job, he continues to trust and serve God. He doesn't blame God, but simply accepts that awful things happen.'

'Well that's not a very satisfactory answer.'

He's right there.

'Who says you deserve a satisfactory answer, Nathan?' Mei raised her eyebrows. 'The world is run according to certain principles, many of which we don't really understand, and most of those we understand we can't control. Illnesses of the body and natural disasters spring to mind. I don't think God chooses who will get cancer, heart disease or dementia. Nor does he choose which communities to destroy with a tsunami or earthquake. These are consequences of the natural processes of our bodies and the world. Yet many people feel the need to blame someone, so they blame God. Some even blame God when they load up on alcohol and crash the car.'

'Mei and I have been victims of random events, or situations we didn't cause.' James looked briefly at Mei. 'We are very grateful for all we have, but our business has struggled from time to time because of political unrest on the other side of the world, because someone wanted to take our big clients, because of an accident when a cable broke, and so on. We can't blame God whenever things happen to interfere with our comfortable lives.'

'I think we'd all like simpler answers to the world's problems and disasters,' Ellie said. 'All I can say is that I don't believe that God wishes ill on people any more than a loving parent would wish ill on their child.'

'I agree, Ellie. All we can do is to trust God's love.' And then Mei launched into a poem. She spoke quietly, as she often does, but we heard every word:

'There is quietness over the hill.
No steel armies, no conflicts,
    but peace —
    peace for the soul,
    incomprehensible,
    for eternity.
How can I know?
There is a hill,
And because of it, peace, freedom, fulfillment, hope,
    are mine —
    now.
Even now:
    amid raging armies of distorted ideals,
    greed,
    hatred,
    perverted minds,
    the ceaseless confusion of empty words.
For me, no fear nor despair:
I know of a hill and one who died there
    to give this peace.
The hill?
You may have heard the name —
Calvary …?'

HEROES

Much later. Satisfied stomachs. For now.

Alex scraped the last scraps of food from the barbecue. Nathan sat back, looking content. 'Great job with the barbecuing, Alex. You're a lucky woman, Jo, to have such a wonderful husband.'

Jo raised her eyebrows and smiled. 'Actually, I am. I don't like cooking steak. I never know when it's ready — you know, not undercooked, not overcooked. I never seem to get it just right.'

'That's what I love about microwave ovens,' said Ellie. 'They're quick, and it's easy to tell when things are cooked.'

'That's because barbecues work from the outside in; microwaves work from the inside out,' explained Nathan, adding, 'Sort of.'

'So God is like a microwave. He works from the inside out.'

'Eh?' James surprised us all again with his way of talking about God.

'Ah,' said James.

'Because God loves us, he wants us to be heroes, people who turn our lives around to become more than we could ever have imagined. So he sent his Spirit to change us from the inside out and make us new people — no matter what we're like inside.'

Alex returned to the circle. 'I thought people changed from the outside. You know, new hair style, tan, teeth …' He laughed.

'Only superficially. We can change our clothes, we can change our appearance, we can even try to change our behaviour, but it's not sustainable, and it's just window-dressing unless we change inside — our attitudes, our ways of thinking, our values.'

'There's an old rhyme about that,' said Ani. 'I think it was written by John Kendrick Bangs, and if I can remember it correctly, it goes:

Some folks in looks take so much pride,

They don't think much on what's inside.

Well, as for me, I know my face

Can ne'er be made a thing of grace,

And so I rather think I'll see

How I can fix th'inside o' me;

So folks'll say, "He looks like sin,

But ain't he beautiful within?"

We all laughed and applauded.

'I get where James is going with this,' said Jo. 'There are people in our community who seem unable to reform their ways no matter what penalty is meted out nor how often. Our prisons provide a penalty for crime and they claim that they try to reform the criminal. Yet courts and prisons are replete with repeat offenders.'

'I agree,' said Mei. 'While people might try to change their patterns of behaviour, unless they change from the inside they fail.'

'How can we change from the inside?' asked Alex, waving one arm dismissively. 'I am who I am. You're who you are. We were born that way or we grew that way and we're too old now to be anyone different.'

'That's a sad and defeatist attitude to life,' said Ellie.

'Well it's true, isn't it? As Jo says, criminals will always be criminals, lazy people will always be lazy, liars will always lie, sarcastic people will always be sarcastic.' He hesitated for a moment, before laughing. 'Look at me. I haven't changed.'

'Do you want to?'

'Nah. I'm happy the way I am.'

'And there's the rub!' James nodded slowly. 'There are people who try to change, but fail, despite making a genuine effort. Enter God. He offers a solution.'

'What solution?' asked Nathan. 'I'm making a list of the things I want Ani to change.'

'Don't mess with perfection.' Ani pointed a finger at him.

'Ah, a solution to both her dissolution and your disillusion.' I gave my most dazzling smile.

'Clever.'

'Thank you.'

James picked up where he left off. 'The solution comes in two parts.'

'Do we have to put it together, like a flatpack?' I don't know where that came from. It's just how my mind works.

'Sometimes I worry about your mind,' said Ellie. 'It flies off in weird directions. You need to see a psych.'

'I did that, but because I'm a mechanic, she made me lie under the couch and fix it.'

Ellie stared at me for a moment, then said, 'You were saying, James?'

James smiled. He never seems to be distracted by our banter. 'Well, first, God lets us start again. He forgives.'

'Ah, the solution is absolution for our dissolution and disillusion.' I was on a roll.

'If you like. God's absolution is complete and unconditional.'

'We're not really used to this, are we?' said Mei. 'People who care about us will forgive us some things, not forgive others. They may be willing to move on without necessarily forgiving. Most of us will be happy if the people we care about simply accept our failings.'

'That's the thing about love.' What is, Ellie? 'We forgive our partner's errors — well, most of them; we draw a line under the past and start again — well, sometimes.'

Just as well, really.

'But that's not always possible,' said Ani. 'Some people cause their partner harm or pain or trauma that damages the relationship irreparably: you know, physical abuse, infidelity, disloyalty, actions which cause irretrievable distrust.'

Mei nodded her agreement. 'But God forgives things that a partner, a friend, even society, might find difficult to forgive. And remember, forgiveness doesn't mean there are no consequences, no punishment. And it doesn't mean we can go on doing the same things.'

James pulled at his nose. 'Life with God is full of new beginnings. It's why Easter is about eggs — the symbol of new life, new beginnings. God makes us feel brand new, not just within ourselves, but in our relationship with him.'

> Because of this decision we don't evaluate people by what they have or how they look. We looked at the Messiah that way once and got it all wrong, as you know. We certainly don't look at him that way anymore. Now we look inside, and what we see is that anyone united with the Messiah gets a fresh start, is created new. The old life is gone; a new life burgeons! Look at it! All this comes from the God who settled the relationship between us and him, and then called us to settle our relationships with each other. God put the world square with himself through the Messiah, giving the world a fresh start by offering forgiveness of sins. God has given us the task of telling everyone what he is doing. We're Christ's representatives. God uses us to persuade men

and women to drop their differences and enter into God's work of making things right between them. We're speaking for Christ himself now: Become friends with God; he's already a friend with you. 'How? you ask. In Christ. God put the wrong on him who never did anything wrong, so we could be put right with God. (2 Corinthians 5: 16–21, MSG)

'But popular psychology tells us to embrace our past, accept who we have become because of it, because many people struggle to deal with past trauma and its impact on who they now are.' Ani was clearly wrestling with this.

'I understand that,' James said gently. 'But despite our best efforts, it's difficult to let go of the past so that it doesn't hold us back. It's difficult to change our present simply by wanting to. It's difficult to create, or even imagine, a new future, built on trying to think or behave differently.' You could almost hear the cogs grinding in people's brains as we considered this. 'But God makes it possible. His Spirit, living within us, changes us from the inside out. Don't underestimate this. Don't gloss over it. God offers a new beginning, a new life, a new future. And, most importantly, a new relationship with him.'

I really like the way James explains things. I decided that I should try to be less flippant and more constructive — really. 'Nicodemus had a similar problem with this. He was a religious leader, who was sincerely trying to understand Jesus' teaching, but had trouble believing Jesus' concept of a new life. He said, you can't re-enter the womb and be born again.'

'Ouch. That conjures images I'd like to erase.'

Just when I'm trying to be serious, Jo is flippant! 'Jesus explained that you don't get born again in the body, but in the Spirit. God remakes you from the inside.'

'You're right Pete,' said James. 'There you have it, succinctly. Jesus offers a new life to those who choose to accept it. Further, it's not a one-off opportunity. When we fail — and God knows we will — he invites us to ask forgiveness, and then begin again.'

Nathan was on his feet, stretching his back. 'That seems unrealistic. For example, a druggie can try to kick it several times, but after a while, people give up on them, and I think they probably give up on themselves.'

'Which highlights the wonder of Christ's offer. It has no limits. We don't get five "get out of jail" vouchers, not even one a month, not even one a week. If we're sincere in seeking his forgiveness, he lets us begin again, as often as it takes. The page is torn from the record book, so that it need not be referred to again. Who else will make you an offer like that?'

'So we just ask for forgiveness. That's it?' Ani looked thoughtful.

'That's it — if you mean it. Like most forgiveness, it helps if we begin with an admission and an apology. That's how we seek forgiveness from the people we love. It's the same with God.'

'He willingly forgives our sins, the things we do which breach the boundaries of our relationship and damage our connection with him,' said Mei. 'As James said earlier, it's called grace, and it's one of the most wonderful things about God.'

'"Amazing grace, how sweet the sound that saved a wretch like me, I once was lost but now am found, was blind but now I see."' I didn't sing it, but I did have more lines to go, when Mei interrupted me.

'Exactly, Pete. John Newton, who wrote that, was a slave trader who had caused untold misery and death to thousands of African slaves. Then he became a Christian. He was amazed that God would forgive him, so he wrote *Amazing grace*.'

You learn something new every day.

Nathan leaned against a post, his back apparently troubling him, poor man. 'Hang on, James. You said that the solution comes in two parts.'

He did. I'd forgotten, and I think the others had too. Nathan must be really following this.

'You said the first part is that God forgives us. What's the second part?'

'Thanks for reminding me, Nathan. The second part is that God gives us his Spirit. It's good to start again, but how do we know we can change? As we said earlier, there are many people who have attempted to rid themselves of addictions or habitual behaviours, but have found themselves falling back into the same patterns. It's not because they don't want to change; it's simply that they can't.'

'I understand the problem, but I don't get the solution.'

'Let me explain it this way: Imagine if every prisoner who really wanted to change was given a companion when they were released, a companion who could not be seduced into crime, and who was with them every hour of every day, advising, encouraging, helping them to live a crime-free life. They would probably go off the rails occasionally, but over time, their typical choices and patterns of behaviour would change, until they adopted a new way of thinking and living. It would probably be a bit invasive, but it might work. God knows that, so he gives us a helper — his Spirit. This Spirit is in us, advising, encouraging, helping us to live a sin-free life. We will probably go off the rails occasionally, but over time, our typical choices and patterns of behaviour will change, until we adopt a new way of thinking and living.'

'A companion who is with us always, but we don't have to buy them dinner or pay their bus fares. Sounds great,' I said.

'And that's what the Spirit is?' Ellie asked.

'Pretty much.'

'What a companion,' said Mei.

WOOING

No idea of the time, but you can guess. Choice of unusual ice cream flavours on sticks. Perhaps I'm not full after all.

Nathan selected an ice cream. 'If God wants people to do the right thing, why doesn't he make them?' He seems to be getting more into these discussions. I chose to get into the ice cream.

'Ah,' said James.

'Because God loves us, he woos us. He doesn't force his attentions on us, but waits for us to respond. At our lowest or highest moments, when we realise we need him, he's there. He always keeps in touch, no matter where we are, although we sometimes miss the signals.'

Mei added, 'God gave us the capacity to think, to consider, to choose. Jesus did not beat people about the head with his message. He warned people about consequences, but he always left them to choose.'

'I think some Christians forget this.' Ellie unwrapped her ice cream, to reveal a coating of smooth chocolate. 'In their passion to share God's message, they leave no room for interpretation and no time for understanding. When confronted with genuine and appropriate questions, they shut down the conversation with a blunt "Because the Bible says so".'

That seemed to strike a chord with Nathan. 'I've met a few of them. I must say, James, that you never answer a question with "Because the Bible says so". Does that mean you don't believe the Bible?'

'To the contrary. The Bible tells me about God and my place in his world. It is the source of my beliefs about Jesus. It describes the basic tenets of my faith. But what we read in the Bible must mesh with our understanding of ourselves, our contemporary world, and God.'

As usual, James got it in a nutshell.

Ellie scanned the group. 'I think that we Christians are sometimes so keen to share how wonderful it is to have God in our lives sometimes that we lose perspective. We can commend our faith to people, but we mustn't coerce them.'

'I agree, Ellie,' said Jo. 'When Christians demand that people follow Christ without sound consideration, they do a disservice to Christ and to the individual. A person who is coerced or manipulated into following Christ will soon lose the enthusiasm when the pressure is off. They won't have a reasoned understanding of faith which they can apply to all of life's situations, but an immature faith which doesn't grow with them.'

Ani nodded gently. 'I'm glad to hear you say that, because I know many people who have been repelled by Christian teaching.'

'Including me.' We all looked at Nathan. 'I attended a Christian school, but my introduction to faith was dogmatic and emphatic, did not allow for exploration and understanding, and was presented by people whose lives didn't inspire me to follow. So I decided Christianity was at best nonsense, at worst fraudulent.'

'I'm sorry to hear that, Nathan.' James' eyes and voice conveyed his sincerity. 'That's not God's way. Jesus will not coerce us to follow. He woos us. Unfortunately, Christ's sales reps do not always represent him well.'

'I like your concept of "wooing" us,' said Jo.

'Is that another word for stalking?' asked Ani.

Mei laughed. 'No. James wooed me.'

'I thought I wowed you.' James reached out and tickled the back of her neck.

'That too — but not until after you had wooed me.' Then to the rest of us she said, 'He was there, keeping in touch, wanting us to get to know one another better, showing kindness and an interest in me. Until, eventually, he wowed me.'

'I think that's a word — and a concept — we've almost lost,' said Jo. 'You can't force someone to love you. You can woo them, but ultimately, love must have the freedom to choose or it is not love. And although people can be attracted, even infatuated, at first sight, love takes time.'

'Meanwhile, they persist.' Ellie looked at me. 'Pete was on the phone or on my doorstep constantly. In the end, I went out with him just to get rid of him.'

'Well that apparently didn't work!' Jo laughed.

I thought I should give my perspective on those events. 'I wasn't going to let her escape. Eventually, she succumbed to my charms.'

'Actually, I discovered that behind the superficial, flippant exterior was a good heart, a good man.'

Oh Ellie. I walked across the group and gave her a kiss, which she returned.

> LORD, you have examined me
> and you know me.
> You know everything I do;
> from far away you understand all my thoughts.
> You see me, whether I am working or resting;
> you know all my actions.
> Even before I speak,
> you already know what I will say.
> You are all around me on every side;
> you protect me with your power.
> Your knowledge of me is too deep;
> it is beyond my understanding.'
> 'Where could I go to escape from you?
> Where could I get away from your presence?
> If I went up to heaven, you would be there;
> if I lay down in the world of the dead, you would be there.

> *If I flew away beyond the east*
> *or lived in the farthest place in the west,*
> *you would be there to lead me,*
> *you would be there to help me.*
> *I could ask the darkness to hide me*
> *or the light around me to turn into night,*
> *but even darkness is not dark for you,*
> *and the night is as bright as the day.*
> *Darkness and light are the same to you. (Psalm 139: 1–12, GNT)*

Alex had been listening to this little exchange. 'I think I remember you saying once before, James, that God wants a relationship with us, and he will keep pursuing us until we catch him. Did I get that right?'

I remember that.

'Probably.' James pulled at his ear.

'Well I like the notion that we can't really escape from God, that he wants a relationship with us, and will keep trying. Like Pete with Ellie.'

'Still sounds a bit like stalking,' said Nathan.

'Not when we are pursued by God.' Mei looked at Nathan. 'Why would we want to be out of sight of the one who cares for us? We are like children. When we are in trouble, or when we don't want to do something we have been told to do, we might try to hide, but we are disappointed if our parents don't come looking for us. We want to know that they care, that they will find us if we need to be found.'

'I've heard people tell how they tried to ignore God's attention,' said Ellie. 'They told themselves, I'm too young; I have goals I'm trying to achieve; I'm too busy; I'm struggling to keep in touch with friends; I'm in love; I'm raising children and that is too full on to think of anything else; my parents got on fine without God; I don't know how or where to begin to find God; anyway, God doesn't care about me … Excuse after excuse. But eventually, they gave in.'

'God comes looking for you because he loves you.' James licked the last of the ice cream from the stick. 'You will never be free of his concern for you. He is unlikely to drop a lightning bolt on you — although there are many people who tell stories of things like that happening to them when they first encountered God.'

'That was Paul's story, wasn't it?' I was keen to show I was still following. 'As he drove to Damascus to arrest Christians, he was struck blind by a flash of light, and Jesus spoke to him, asking why Paul was persecuting him.'

'Absolutely,' said Ellie. 'It turned Paul's life around. He went from prosecuting Christians to preaching about Christ, travelling throughout the known world. The Bible contains a record of his adventures, which were impressive and exciting for his time.'

'He must have accumulated plenty of frequent flyer points.' I just can't help myself.

She ignored me. 'He also spent time in prisons, spoke with world leaders, and wrote letters which contain great teaching about the gospel.'

James stroked the side of his face. 'While all that is true, we mustn't assume that everyone will have a "blinding flash" experience. There are many other ways in which God will remind you that he is still there, still waiting until you are ready. Sooner or later, through a desperate situation or a gentle one, by stark means or subtle, you may recognise and meet God. The time will come when you will look for him. And when you do, he'll be there.'

'Just don't wait too long,' added Mei quietly, 'because you're missing out on life.'

COMMITMENT

It's late, but no-one seems to care. Coffee? Please. Just no more food.

'I wonder how many followers Jesus would have on his social media accounts if he was here today.' Where did that come from, Alex? I'm not the only one whose mind drifts strangely.

'But he *is* here.' Quick retort, Mei.

'I meant if he was walking around and doing TV spots and podcasts and blogs and all that. He'd have billions.'

'Perhaps. But I don't think that would have impressed him.'

'Why not? You would think that Jesus would be happy to accept everyone who wanted to follow him.' Standing by the coffee pot, Alex waved his coffee cup dangerously. We all hoped it was still empty. 'After all, the more followers you have to your social media account, the more credible you are seen to be and the more you are listened to.'

'Yes, but "following" Jesus is not simply about reading tweets and blogs. He wants commitment.'

'Everyone wants commitment, but not everyone is willing to give it.' Jo screwed up her nose.

'That reminds me,' I said. 'I must talk to Arun.'

'Don't you dare.' Ellie responded quickly. 'He and Gabby have their heads screwed on. They'll deal with it when they're ready.'

'Jesus understands how you feel,' said James. 'He was all about commitment.'

'It's not the way to get followers.' As usual, Alex gesticulated as he spoke. We were still concerned about the coffee cup, which was now full. 'These days, you sign them up, try to hang onto them with regular communications, and hope for sales later.'

'But it's a one-way street. Followers may give loyalty, but they don't get it. The celebrities don't know who they are, couldn't care about them, as long as they can publicise their concerts or books or recordings or make advertising money from them.'

'I've never thought of it like that. Nathan placed his coffee cup on the table. 'So how does this relate to Jesus?'

'He's the first to commit,' said James. 'He hopes for commitment in return.'

'What do you mean?'

'Ah,' said James.

'Because God loves us, he has no problem with commitment — he gives it, he expects it. He didn't desert us when Jesus left earth. His humanity wasn't a passing interest or a failed experiment. He left us with his Spirit, so that he is always present. He's committed.'

'But he still wants people to commit to him, right?'

'Absolutely,' said James, 'but Jesus wants people to follow him knowing the cost. He doesn't pretend that it will be easy. He challenges people to understand the implications for their own lives. He even dismissed some followers who he felt weren't really understanding the consequences of their decision.'

> *One day one of the local officials asked him, "Good Teacher, what must I do to deserve eternal life?"*
>
> *[19-20] Jesus said, "Why are you calling me good? No one is good — only God. You know the commandments, don't you? No illicit sex, no killing, no stealing, no lying, honour your father and mother."*
>
> *[21] He said, "I've kept them all for as long as I can remember."*

> ²² When Jesus heard that, he said, "Then there's only one thing left to do: Sell everything you own and give it away to the poor. You will have riches in heaven. Then come, follow me."
> ²³ This was the last thing the official expected to hear. He was very rich and became terribly sad. He was holding on tight to a lot of things and not about to let them go. (Matthew 18: 18–23, MSG)

'Jo commented that people these days seem unwilling to commit to relationships.' Ellie smiled across the table at her. 'She's right. When it becomes difficult, they bail out. Yet relationships go through difficult times. Breaking up may be difficult, but sometimes, staying together is even more difficult.'

'So what's the secret to a long relationship?' Alex characteristically used his hands to imply that his question probably had no answer. 'How do some people stay married for 50 years or more?' asked Alex.

Ellie had an answer. 'Commitment. Intent. They made a decision to stay together as husband and wife for life, so parting is not an option. Right Pete?'

That put me on the spot, so I quickly agreed. But then, I thought for a moment.

As I hesitated, Nathan said, 'He's afraid he might say something he hasn't thought of yet.'

'He who hesitates may not be lost, but he'll probably get interrupted.' Then I said, 'Seriously, over time, people change, circumstances change, society changes. We are not the people we were when we married. Our circumstances are not what they were or what we expected them to be. While we are totally smitten by our lover, it's easy to promise "for better, for worse, for richer, for poorer, in sickness and in health, to love and to cherish till death do us part", but change sometimes pulls people apart.

Commitment keeps them together, the agreement that they will see it through and the determination to make it work, no matter what.'

'Like God,' said James. He did it again. 'He doesn't blow hot and cold. He doesn't love us according to how we behave or how we relate to him. He loves us no matter what. He's committed to us no matter what. He'll stay with us no matter what. In return, he hopes for the same commitment from us.'

Ellie frowned. 'I find that there are times I feel very close to God and times when he seems to be distant; times when I feel very content in my relationship with him and times when I feel he's ignoring or rejecting me; times when following him is a delight and times when it all seems too hard.'

'Sounds a bit like marriage.' Jo grinned.

There was some laughter, and a few remarks made. I decided it was better to stay quiet.

'I understand, Jo.' James wrapped his hands around his cup. 'God knows and accepts that, but he expects our commitment, a willingness to see it through, an intention to stick together for life.'

'Sounds even more like marriage.' Alex blew a kiss to Jo.

'James said earlier that, through his Spirit, God enters our lives, changing us from the inside. He becomes a part of who we are, shaping our actions by shaping our thinking. Further, he is sometimes called the comforter, the one who helps us, advises us, supports us — in other words, the Spirit provides us with whatever we need in our lives.' Mei smiled. 'Now that's a deal you won't get elsewhere!'

LOVE

Later still. A cheese board. Do we really need anything else to eat? I don't think so, but I don't want to appear ungrateful.

The cheese board was passed around, and the conversation drifted. Then Ani brought us back to our conversation about faith. 'You Christians are big on love.'

I guess we are.

But Mei nailed it. 'That's because God is big on love. So big that Jesus says "God is love". God doesn't just love; he *is* love. It is the core of his nature. He defines love.'

Nathan wasn't convinced. 'Love is just mushy feelings. How can God have mushy feelings?'

'Ah,' said James.

'Because God loves us, he showed us that love is more than mushy feelings. He sacrificed for us. He wants us to love other people that way too.'

'But I like the mushy feelings.' Ani tilted her head. 'Wobbly stomach, aching feeling somewhere inside, shaky legs, dizzy head, clumsy actions, weird smile, awkward conversation.' She hesitated. 'Well, I used to.'

'I get that,' said Mei. 'Love shapes our feelings, making us yearn and desire; it dominates our thinking, cluttering our thoughts; it inspires our dreaming, giving us images of the future. But if it goes no further, then it is fantasy. The one we love will never know, and we will never have a loving relationship with them. Only through action will they know that we love them and want a relationship with them. Only through action will they learn to believe our love, trust our love, rely on our love and reciprocate our love.'

Wow. We were all silent for a moment as we thought about that.

'Beautifully put, Mei. I'm glad I married you.' James gave Mei a wonderful, sincere smile, which she reciprocated. Then James added, 'Our love for God, too, can shape our feelings, dominate our thoughts, and inspire our dreaming. But it also must go beyond that to affect our actions.'

I guess that makes sense.

Ellie elaborated. 'Jesus explained that we show our love for him when we show our love for people. He told a story in which he explained that when we show love to people, we are showing love to God. When we feed the hungry, visit prisoners, show kindness to strangers, and so on, it's like we are doing it for him.'

> '... I was hungry and you gave me something to eat, I was thirsty and you gave me something to drink, I was a stranger and you invited me in, I needed clothes and you clothed me, I was sick and you looked after me, I was in prison and you came to visit me.'
>
> 'Then the righteous will answer him, 'Lord, when did we see you hungry and feed you, or thirsty and give you something to drink? When did we see you a stranger and invite you in, or needing clothes and clothe you? When did we see you sick or in prison and go to visit you?'
>
> 'The King will reply, 'Truly I tell you, whatever you did for one of the least of these brothers and sisters of mine, you did for me.' (Matthew 25: 35–46, NIV)'

'So if you pass me some of that cheese, you'll be doing it for God, right Ellie?' I thought this was a good line.

'I try to do everything for God, Pete.'

I didn't have an answer for that.

Mei saved me. 'We Christians aren't perfect. We don't always behave as we should. We sometimes lose our way, lose our perspective, lose our vision of Jesus. We are seduced by temptations around us. We respond to the circumstances of our lives, to our relationships, to our own moods and emotions in ways that we sometimes regret, or even in ways that we know at the time to be wrong. Put bluntly, we're human.'

'It sounds like an elaborate excuse to me,' said Nathan. 'Christians ought to be better than that, because they have made a commitment — that was the word you used — to serve God and to follow the teachings of Jesus. And you say they have God's help to do that. What would be the point of following a Christian leader if they're no better than me?'

Mei agreed. 'Of course you're right, Nathan. However, the fact remains that we sometimes fall short of God's standards, and even our own. But you can take comfort in the fact that we Christians don't follow other Christians; we follow Christ. Christians fail; Christ doesn't.'

'But people follow their favourite preacher, or some Christian celebrity, don't they?' asked Alex.

'Some do. I suppose it's easy for any of us to be so impressed by a person's wisdom or charisma that we find ourselves following them. It happened in the early church too, and Paul explained that it was wrong. He didn't want people to follow church leaders — not even him. He wanted them to follow Christ.'

> *For some people from Chloe's family have told me quite plainly, my friends, that there are quarrels among you. Let me put it this way: each one of you says something different. One says, "I follow Paul"; another, "I follow Apollos"; another, "I follow Peter"; and another, "I follow Christ." Christ has been divided into groups! Was it Paul who died on the cross for you? Were you*

baptised as Paul's disciples? (1 Corinthians 1: 11–13, GNT)

'I think the key here, Alex,' explained James, 'is that if you know a Christian preacher or teacher who assists you with your faith, then by all means listen to them. If there's a Christian whose life seems to be a model of Christian living, watch them. If there is a church where you feel you connect and are helped in your faith, attend there. But always remember that we follow Christ, not other people, that our example is Christ. If the Christians you admire let you down, don't blame Christ. Support them, if you are able, reminding them that our challenge is to be the best that we can be in our service for God.'

'That's a goal worth pursuing,' said Mei, quietly.

BECAUSE GOD WANTS TO HELP US ... HE GIVES US A SUPPORT CREW

It's all very well to know that God loves us and wants a relationship with us, but living God's way can be difficult. We struggle to be the people we know we ought to be. Even the great missionary, Paul, whose 2000-year-old letters are still useful today, admitted that he sometimes did what he shouldn't and struggled to do what he should. So what hope do we have? To add to the difficulty, Jesus left his followers with instructions to spread his teachings, and to model his formula for living, even in the face of opposition.

Are we really up to it? Has God set us up to fail? What was he thinking?

It's simple really. Because God wants to help us, he gives us a support crew.

Let me show you.

FAMILY

May 11: Post-Easter. The usual drinks and gossip, this time at our home again. Typical late autumn night. Cold, but clear, so we're outside as usual. Soup to warm us.

Gabby is living at home again, so she asked if she could join us. Surprisingly, Arun asked to join in too. It's good to have them. I find their company stimulating. During the usual conversation to hear the latest in one another's lives, Ellie asked, 'So did you go to church at Easter, Nathan?'

'No, but I assume you did.'

'Of course. I like my church. I find it very helpful.'

'I think you'd be one of the few.'

'Far more than you might imagine, Nathan. Billions throughout the world. What's your problem with church?'

'You know my problem. People who go to church are hypocrites. They talk a good game, but they don't play it.' Then he quickly added, 'Well, most of them. Present company excepted.'

'I know a few like that.' Nathan showed surprise at Ellie's openness. 'But then, you could say that's why they go to church.'

'Eh?'

I'm with you, Nathan. Eh?

'Well church isn't for the perfect. It's for the growing.'

'I don't get it.'

'Faith isn't a possession. It's a process. We don't "get faith" and then that's it. It's not a tattoo — something stamped on the skin or the psyche, and then that's it for all time. Faith is a process of being changed by God — daily, weekly, annually … People go to church to help one another with the process.' This woman continues to amaze me. I feel a bit inadequate.

'I thought you had to believe everything to go to church,' said Ani.

'Christians have doubt,' said Ellie.'

Mei nodded. 'Yes, me too.'

Really? I would never have thought that. Mei is so calm and articulate when she speaks about faith. I noticed that James was also nodding gently. What, him too?

Mei continued. 'Doubt is a component of faith, not the opposite to faith. It's like the share market — up one day, down the next, a series of peaks and troughs. Faith is being faithful, through all the peaks and troughs.'

'Nathan grounded us again. 'Well, that's all very elucidating, and it apparently works for you, but I'm not good enough to go to church.'

Ellie laughed. 'And you think that Pete is? You don't know him very well.' I thought that a little unkind.

'I think you've fallen for a common misunderstanding about the church.' James pulled gently at the hair behind his ear. 'Many people who are not part of a church community think that the church building is where good people gather to celebrate their goodness. Nothing could be further from the truth. People gather in church buildings because they are very aware of their failings; because they know that they do not always live as Jesus commands, creating a distance between them and God; because they want to say sorry to God and learn how to live better lives for him; because they want to connect with other people who feel the same way, to encourage and help one another.'

'The church is for sinners, not for the perfect,' explained Mei.

Ellie looked at me. 'So Pete fits right in.' Again, a little unkind, I thought. But then she laughed. 'Of course, I'm only joking. As Mei says, the church is for sinners, and that's all of us.'

'Because you said earlier, James, that a sinner is anyone who doesn't meet God's expectations,' said Ani. 'Right?'

'Spot on, Ani. And, as Ellie has pointed out, we all fall short in our relationship with God: we neglect to spend time with God; we fail to follow Jesus' example; we do things we know are contrary to what Jesus taught…'

'And that's all before breakfast!' This time I got a bit of a laugh.

'Each of these things chips away at our relationship with God,' said James. 'We repair it by acknowledging our neglect, saying sorry, and making an effort to do better.'

'It's not unlike our relationships with people,' said Mei. 'Sometimes we neglect them when they need our attention; we say things — intentionally or not — that are hurtful; we leave them to do things we should assist them with; we put our own needs before theirs; we don't encourage them when they need it …'

'And that's all before morning tea!' Well, *I* thought it was funny.

'Each of these acts chips away at our relationship with them. We repair it by acknowledging our neglect, saying sorry, and making an effort to do better.'

'I think Christians who go to church are self-congratulatory. They think they are perfect and others don't meet their standards.' Nathan has told us about his experience with hypocritical Christians, and it's left its mark on him.

'Well interestingly,' said James, 'that's not what Jesus was like. He was criticised on one occasion for mixing with prostitutes, collaborators, criminals, and other "undesirables". His response was to say that people who are well and healthy don't need a doctor. He came to help people who did. Although he healed people, he wasn't referring to people's physical health, but their spiritual and emotional health.'

> After this, Jesus went out and saw a tax collector named Levi, sitting in his office. Jesus said to him, 'Follow me.' Levi got up, left everything, and followed him.
>
> Then Levi had a big feast in his house for Jesus, and among the guests was a large number of tax collectors

> and other people. Some Pharisees and some teachers of the Law who belonged to their group complained to Jesus' disciples. 'Why do you eat and drink with tax collectors and other outcasts?' they asked.
>
> Jesus answered them, 'People who are well do not need a doctor, but only those who are sick. I have not come to call respectable people to repent, but outcasts.'
> (Luke 5: 27–32, GNT)

James continued. 'Jesus chose to help those who needed help and knew it. When people attend church, they do it because they need help and they know it.'

'I think some Christians are very strange,' said Ani.

I smirked. 'Present company excepted.'

She hesitated. 'Not necessarily.' But she returned a cheesy smile.

'People are people. Some of them are like us — and therefore "normal" — and some are not — and therefore, "strange".' Nailed it, Ellie. 'But if we have a relationship with someone, we accept them for who they are, with all their quirks.' She paused and smiled at me. 'And some are quirkier than others, aren't they darling.'

I gave her my warmest smile. 'And we accept their family, too,' I said. 'When we love someone, we want them to meet the other people who matter to us, including our family.' I turned to Arun and Gabby, who had been silent during our discussion. 'Is that right, Arun?'

'Of course. And I'm honoured to be invited.' He is very good at saying the right thing.

'I can only apologise for my family, Arun,' said Gabby. 'They are a bit strange. And embarrassing.'

Arun laughed. 'Every family has its embarrassing members. You've yet to meet all of my crowd: You know that Mum can be a bit effusive in her welcome; my young brother Jacob will probably play an embarrassing practical joke; Nanna Joy will probably take out her teeth; older sister Kara is likely to conduct an interrogation; Uncle Bert is likely to make some inappropriate joke.'

'Like God says — "Love me, love my family."' We all looked at James. He just comes out with these things without warning.

'Do you want to elaborate on that, James?' asked Ellie.

'Ah,' said James.

'Because God loves us, he wants us to be part of his family. Like most families, it's a weird mix: some we like, some we'd rather avoid. But, like it or not, they're family.'

'How did we get from weird families to God?' asked Alex. 'I'm still thinking about Jo's family. There are some stories there.' Jo thumbed her nose at him.

'God has a family too,' said James. 'We call it the church. Like most families, it includes a range of personalities, including some who embarrass us, some we would prefer to avoid and some we gravitate towards. Like most families, there are members scattered all over the world, some of whom we may rarely or never meet. But they're family. They matter because they care about us, celebrate with us when we have successes, support us when we struggle, help us through difficult times, assist us to make difficult decisions, teach us about life, share their own experiences to guide us, sacrifice for us … And we have a responsibility to do the same for them. Perhaps it can be explained this way …'

And then, to everyone's surprise, he began to sing — a bit country and western meets blues meets stand-up comedy — even though he stayed sitting down:

> 'My father used to say, "Son, you can choose your
>   friends your way,
> But when it comes to family, I'm afraid you get no say;
> For God has given you to us and he's given us to you

To care for one another, and there's nothing you can do."
Well let me tell you all it's the same with you and me:
We didn't choose each other but we're all a family.
When God made me his child, and made you his child too,
That made us a family to care as families do.

'My father used to say, "Son, we're a funny lot it's true.
We're each an individual, though I've grown mad like you.
But families are just like that — we're each of us unique,
But we complement each other and that makes us strong not weak."
Well let me tell you all it's the same with you and me:
We're each an individual, but we're all a family.
When God made me his child and made you his child too,
That made us a family to care as families do.'

'My father used to say, "Son, you've relatives galore!
Though you may not have seen them, you know that there are more.
They're scattered all around the world living life their way,
Each carrying on the family name in their own special way."
Well let me tell you all it's the same with you and me:
Known by the name of Christian we're all a family.
When God made me his child and made you his child too,
That made us a family to care as families do.'

There was a burst of spontaneous applause and complimentary comments. James never ceases to amaze me.

'Family. We love 'em,' said Mei.

CELEBRATIONS

Later. The familiar sound and aroma of the barbecue.

'I'm not part of this family,' said Arun, 'but I have some questions about the church.' I like this young man. He has some depth. Reminds me of myself. Although I'm not yet used to the idea of someone being in love with my daughter.

'Fire away,' said James.

'You go to church, right?'

'Sure do. Because I'm a Christian I'm part of the church, but I also go to church.'

'Why?'

'Because we're family, we like to get together from time to time.'

'Depends on your family. As you said in your song, some are weird. An occasional gathering is plenty.'

'True. The difference with the church family is that we don't just get together to please ourselves. We do it to please God.'

'It is sometimes called worship or celebration,' added Mei. 'We meet to praise and thank God together, to get with others who want to say, "Hooray for God!"'

'Hooray for God! I've never heard that. I thought it was all about sermons, rituals, candles and other paraphernalia. And all very sombre. How come you see it differently?'

'Ah,' said James.

'Because God loves his family, he loves to see us celebrating his love together, and I don't think he's too fussed about how we do it.'

Mei elaborated. 'Time spent with my church family is not about those activities; it's about the meaning behind them. Why we do things is more important than what we do. Anything can be done in church that helps to bring meaning, that helps us to connect with God.'

Ellie added, 'And why is also more important than where. Christians meet in homes, halls, schools, parks, beaches, shops … wherever is convenient.'

'The purpose of the church celebration is to grow closer to God and closer to friends in the Christian community.' James rubbed the end of his nose.

> *Welcome with open arms fellow believers who don't see things the way you do. And don't jump all over them every time they do or say something you don't agree with — even when it seems that they are strong on opinions but weak in the faith department. Remember, they have their own history to deal with. Treat them gently. …*
>
> *Cultivate your own relationship with God, but don't impose it on others. You're fortunate if your behaviour and your belief are coherent. But if you're not sure, if you notice that you are acting in ways inconsistent with what you believe — some days trying to impose your opinions on others, other days just trying to please them — then you know that you're out of line. If the way you live isn't consistent with what you believe, then it's wrong. (Romans 14: 1, 22-23, MSG)*

'So long, boring sermons are not compulsory?'

'Of course not.' Mei was struggling to cut a piece of meat. 'Sometimes they are very entertaining, and always informative. We hear teaching about God, and share insights and stories about faith.'

'Where does prayer come in?'

'Let me.' Jo likes to share her thoughts, and it's always interesting. 'Prayer is conversation with God. Through prayer, we acknowledge God, thank him for all the good things in our lives, and say sorry for our failings; and we tell him our concerns — for ourselves and other people, and ask him to help …'

Nathan interrupted. 'What's the point. Nothing changes.'

'Actually it does,' said Jo. 'It changes me. And sometimes God intervenes and changes things.'

'Not always.'

'No, not always.'

'Why does God sometimes do what you pray for and sometimes not?' Arun appeared too absorbed to eat from the plate before him.

'I don't know why God intervenes in some things and not others. But God's not my magic genie. He is God. It's not his job to meet my expectations. It's my job to meet his.'

I thought that was pretty profound, and said so. 'That was pretty profound, Jo.'

'So tell me about the strange rituals.' This young man had a head full of questions. I think I'll let someone else answer this one.

James put down a chop he was gnawing, and reached for a napkin to wipe his hands. 'Because God knows that some people like — even need — a bit of theatre, we sometimes include it in our worship too. There are many practices that have developed over centuries to add meaning to worship. However, lots of contemporary churches have created their own ways of worshipping: instead of people waiting in silence, there is a hubbub of greetings; the leaders wear contemporary street wear or business wear; contemporary songs are sung to the amplified sound of a rock band — who probably have a recording contract; words, images and video clips are projected on giant screens; stage and theatre lighting may be used to add effect.'

'But there are some rituals which are part of the life of most Christian churches, and which are so significant that they are often referred to as sacraments or ordinances,' said Mei. 'Like baptism.'

'What's baptism?'

'Baptism is a public expression of commitment to God. Many churches follow the example of John the Baptist and the early church in baptising people by immersing them completely — but just briefly.' Mei smiled. 'It can take place in the ocean, a river, a lake, or a special facility within the church building. Other churches practise infant baptism. Clearly a baby or child cannot make the decision to commit their lives to following Christ, so the parents do this on their behalf, promising to help them learn about God and to nurture their spiritual growth until the child is old enough to make their own commitment. Some churches believe that either is acceptable if it helps people in their faith.'

'And the Lord's supper? What's that?'

'Shortly before Jesus' arrest, he had a meal with his closest disciples. At the end of this meal he shared some bread and wine with them.'

'Is this the thing about drinking Jesus' blood?' Ani screwed up her nose. 'I've never quite understood that.'

'He wasn't speaking literally,' said James. 'Jesus often spoke in metaphors. He was saying that the bread and wine — presumably red wine — represented his body and blood, and that his body was going to be broken and his blood spilled. So he urged his disciples to get together and share a similar meal from time to time, because he knew that this would help them to remember how he lived, how he died, and how he had returned to life — although at this stage they didn't know this was going to happen.'

'So Christians still celebrate this symbolic meal. It isn't much as meals go…' Mei lifted her plate. 'Not like this. It's usually just a small piece of bread or wafer, and a sip of wine, usually non-alcoholic. But it could be pizza and cola; the choice of elements is not critical. What matters is that it is about sharing with other Christians the memory of

Jesus' life and death. It evokes feelings of sorrow, because of what Jesus went through; of joy, because he proved himself to be God and because he has brought purpose to our lives; of reflection, because we confess our sin to God and re-commit ourselves to serving him as well as we are able; and of celebration, because we gather with other people who share our understandings and our feelings about Jesus.'

'I've been in churches where I wasn't supposed to share Communion because I wasn't from that Church organisation,' said Mei.

'Did they ask to see your driver's license?' I asked.

'Not quite, but it's wrong, in my opinion.'

'Why?' asked Arun. 'A church should be allowed to make rules about who comes and who does what, shouldn't they?'

'I don't think they should.' Alex surprised me with that comment, but he explained further. 'I know my attendance at church is a bit erratic, but a church is not a club; it's a community. Clubs have rules to keep people out; communities have rules that welcome people in.'

'Brilliantly put, Alex,' said Ellie. 'No particular church organisation owns the Lord's supper. It's a celebration that Jesus told all his disciples to participate in regularly. So if I think of myself as a disciple, a follower and learner of Jesus, then I am free to celebrate communion with any other followers.' I could see she felt a bit passionate about this.

'In our church, and many others,' I said, 'children participate in Communion alongside their parents, because it's a family meal — the church family, that is.'

Gabby nodded. 'And I always liked that. It made me feel like I really was part of the church family.'

'I agree with that idea.' James scratched behind his ear. 'To exclude some people is like telling them they can come to Christmas lunch but can't eat anything!'

Arun thought for a moment, before asking, 'Why are weddings and funerals held in churches?'

'Because we're family, we celebrate the big moments together,' said James. 'And although these aren't exclusively Christian events, Christians believe that they have Christian significance. We believe that marriage is a declaration of love and commitment made in front of witnesses and before God, so the vows are not to be made lightly.'

'What about funerals?' asked Arun.

'Because Christians believe that there is something more after death, funerals are conducted before God. Sometimes people have difficulty letting go of someone who has died …'

I put my hands around my throat and gasped, 'Let me go. I'm dead. I can't be here anymore!' It didn't get the appreciative response I had hoped for.

James smiled and shook his head slowly, before continuing. 'At a Christian funeral, the mourners pass the deceased into God's hands. There's a sense in which that's something to be happy about. In addition, they believe in God's power to help with their grieving, and they believe in God's forgiveness for anything they might regret about their relationship with the deceased.'

Nathan had been surprisingly quiet. It's funny how we each seem to find some topics that we really engage with, and some we don't, although I think that sometimes there a lot happening behind the eyeballs. 'I don't go to church because I don't want the church telling me what to do.'

Ani agreed. 'Nor do I.'

Jo surprised them both by saying, 'I don't want the church telling me what to do either. I don't serve the church; I serve God.'

'Unfortunately, our understanding of the church has been distorted over the years,' said James. 'The "church" is simply a group name for all the people who believe that Jesus was God on earth, and who are earnestly striving to follow Jesus and live as God requires. Unfortunately, some churches like to be authoritative, backing up their teaching by giving instructions to the members about what they can and can't do in all sorts of areas of their lives.'

'Interestingly, that was one of the complaints Jesus had about the Jewish religious leaders in his time.'

'Spot on, Pete,' said Mei. High praise indeed. 'We haven't learnt, have we?'

'To be fair, generally speaking, churches which are authoritative initially just wanted to help people to know what God expects of them. Their motives weren't necessarily meant to be repressive.' James always looks for the positive in people. I admire that.

'That's true,' said Ellie. 'In the letters which Paul, Peter, John and others wrote to groups of early Christians, the writers often gave instructions about how the people should behave. They weren't trying to be bossy. They were just trying to explain the practical implications of being a Christian. They pointed out that you can't be a Christian and go on behaving the way you did before. When your heart changes, so do your actions.'

I thought that was pretty well put.

'I think you have to realise that, over the centuries, individual churches joined with others with a similar way of thinking to form bigger "churches",' said Ellie. 'I think that some grew so big that the organisation developed a life of its own, dominating the lives of the people and protecting the organisation at any cost from criticism and threat. In recent times, we've heard far too many stories about church organisations placing their survival ahead of the safety and welfare of individuals. There are small churches, too, where a charismatic individual has twisted the purpose and activities of the organisation to their own end.'

'Perhaps these events will cause all churches to consider whether they are accurately expressing the teachings and example of Jesus.' Perhaps so, Mei.

Ani placed her plate on the table. 'I don't get all the stuff that Christians believe.'

Obviously, I do. But I was hoping no-one was going to ask me. Fortunately, James had an answer. 'There are creeds which have been written which provide a summary. But, put simply, Christians believe that there is a creator God. They believe that Jesus was God's son, who showed us how to live, died to enable us to have direct communication with God, and rose again to show that he was God and that death is not the end. We believe that as Spirit, God enters our lives, changing us and helping us to live God's way. We believe that the Bible provides us with the blueprint for life because it contains truths about God. And we believe that the church is the collection of people throughout the world who follow Christ, so it's his church, not ours. Our faith impacts our lives, so that we try to live our lives the way Jesus modelled.

'If Christians all believe the same thing, why are there different churches?' Young Arun is persistent, but I must admit, they're sensible questions.

'While Christians agree on the basics of Christian belief, individuals and groups might emphasise particular beliefs and how Christians should worship or behave.'

'Some become passionate about it, accusing other Christians of being "wrong" in their faith.' That has always annoyed me.

James too, apparently. 'And that's not helpful to anyone.'

Mei took it a step further. 'And unfortunately, the media often focuses more on these differences of opinions than on the beliefs Christians have in common.'

'I think it is reasonable to be confident in what we believe. It is not reasonable to insist that others believe exactly what we do.' Jo spoke with conviction. 'That is fundamentalism: the assumption that everything we believe is right and true and everyone who disagrees with us is therefore wrong. The extension of this stance is that people who disagree with us must be punished in some way. People of several religions, including Christianity, have been guilty of this over the centuries.'

'So how did you decide what church to go to?' asked Ani, who had been surprisingly quiet.

'We cannot choose who is part of our family, but we can choose who we interact with, and who we develop closest relationships with.' James scratched his cheek. 'In the same way, we cannot choose who is in the church family, but we can choose which groups of family members we interact most closely with, by finding a church where we feel connected and helped with our faith. That's what Mei and I did.'

'And we've grown to love them,' added Mei, 'even the weird ones.'

WORDS

Later. Funny weather. Might rain. Empty plates are accumulating on the table.

Arun hasn't yet had all his questions answered. 'And what's with the Bible? Why are Christians always talking about the Bible?'

I'm a little embarrassed to say that Arun is asking questions I don't often think about. I just assume the answers are there, somewhere.

'Ah,' said James.

'Because God loves us, he was prepared to put it in writing. He didn't just flick us a text or emoji, but put together a book. And because he knew that we have different tastes in reading, he put in something for everyone: history, narrative, folk story, poetry, philosophy, predictions, letters, dreams … And as soon as we figured out the internet, he made it available to pretty much everyone, even if they can't read.'

'So God invented the internet?' asked Ani.

'Probably.' James smiled. 'Perhaps he was just waiting for us to work it out.'

'Previous generations wrote letters,' said Jo. 'I would have liked that. The recipient of love letters often held on to them for decades, perhaps re-visiting them from time to time, especially if their loved one was away or had died. It enabled them to relive the moments, relive the feelings.' She pretended to wipe a tear from her eye.

'I think God understood that,' said Ellie. 'That's why we have the Bible.'

'Like letters from a lover, we can read passages from the Bible over and over.' Nicely put, Jo.

Mei agreed. 'There are passages I revisit when I feel down, or need to make a decision, or feel lost and confused, or grieve, or are faced with an opportunity, or when my heart is overflowing with joy, or … You get the idea!'

James added, 'And although each book of the Bible was written by a particular person at a particular time and in a particular setting and culture, its truths about God stand for all time and all places. The Bible is written in men's words, but it is God's Word.'

> *There's nothing like the written Word of God for showing you the way to salvation through faith in Christ Jesus. Every part of Scripture is God-breathed and useful one way or another — showing us truth, exposing our rebellion, correcting our mistakes, training us to live God's way. Through the Word we are put together and shaped up for the tasks God has for us. (2 Timothy 3: 15–17, MSG)*

Arun was still struggling with this. 'But the Bible is an intimidating read.'

Ani was even less enamoured. 'Don't get me started. It's impossible.'

'Well go on. Get started!' I said.

'All right.' Ani took a breath. 'The language is out of date. It's worse than reading Shakespeare.'

'Not any more,' I said. 'The Bible was written in Hebrew and Greek. A widely adopted early English translation was the King James version. It reads like Shakespeare because it was published early in the seventeenth century. But in recent times, the Bible has been translated into contemporary language. You can read it in everyday English in a range of translations, and in almost every other language in the world — online and free.' [1]

'I can't read a book that long!' Alex passed his empty plate to Jo, who placed it on the table.

'We know, darling. But you can also get audio versions of the Bible — again, online and free!'

'It is certainly long,' I said. 'I've tried to read it from cover to cover. And frankly, much of it is extremely boring — when it lists chapter after chapter of laws, for example.'

'It is an intimidating read,' agreed James, 'so I would say that people approaching it for the first time should focus on the New Testament. The new agreement is not a set of laws, but good news. The first four books — Matthew, Mark, Luke and John — tell that good news, which is story of Jesus and what that means for us. Each writer recorded what he saw personally or heard from others, and each wrote for a different audience, so they chose different parts of the story to highlight.'

'I like this because it's just as reporters do nowadays.' Ellie accidentally kicked her plate which was at her feet. Picking it up, she handed it to me. 'You can hear three reports of the same incident and almost wonder if the reporters were at the same event! None has lied, but each has chosen different things to highlight.'

James ran his hand along the side of his neck. 'The next book, the Acts of the Apostles, tells the story of the early Church, and what happened as people spread the story of Jesus and carried on the work that Jesus started. It was written by the same Luke who wrote one of the gospels. Then you will find a sequence of letters, written by leaders in

---

[1] Within this book, there are Biblical quotes from three of those translations (see the printer's details at the beginning of the book), but there are also others. At https://www.biblegateway.com you can read or listen to the Bible in any of a range of versions — free!'

the early church to Christians in Rome, Corinth, Ephesus, Thessaloniki, and so on.'

'But they're real places.' Nathan showed surprise. 'We've been there on a cruise of the Mediterranean.'

I was surprised by his surprise. 'Of course. They were real places 2000 years ago too. Did you think someone made them up?'

'Frankly, yes,' said Nathan.

I continued to be surprised — not that Nathan and Ani had cruised the Mediterranean, but that Nathan should think these places were made up. I always thought him so open-minded and intelligent.

Mei saved us from an awkwardness. 'Early missionaries, like Paul, travelled from Palestine into what we now know as Turkey and Greece and Italy and beyond, telling the good news of Jesus. Groups of people formed local church communities in people's homes. The letters helped the Christians as they tried to live this new life, with its new ways of relating to God and people.'

'What significance would that have for us?' asked Nathan.

'Although written 2000 years ago, their difficulties are very similar to ours,' said Jo. 'How should we worship; how should we behave; how do we deal with conflict and disagreement; what traditions should we continue and what should we change? The issues are the same as we face now, and the insights offered are still useful to us.'

'I like to read the Psalms.' I really do and I explained why. 'They are songs written about God or to God, and although they were written thousands of years ago, I love their raw emotion. The writers accuse God of not listening, passionately plead for help, or encourage God to punish the writer's enemies. Some overflow with praise and gratitude for God's creation, care and faithfulness. Some make deals with God, explaining what great servants of God they'll be if God does what they ask. Some reflect on how well God knows us. In the language and context of the time, the Psalms express the same kinds of feelings about God that we do — without apology and without polite editing.'

'I get that, Pete.' Ellie smiled at me. 'You expressed it perfectly.'

'I tried reading bits of the Bible, but I couldn't make sense of it. It was disjointed, and didn't flow.'

'It appears that way for good reason, Ani.' James scratched at his nose. 'It was written by many different people over hundreds of years. And as I indicated earlier, it's not simply a narrative, but includes various genres.'

'So how do you make sense of that?' Ani was looking puzzled. 'Even books of short stories have some kind of theme or connection.'

'So does the Bible. The Bible makes sense when we realise that it is actually just one story.'

'One story?' Nathan scratched his head. 'You just said it was a mishmash of writings.'

James responded graciously, as usual. 'The Bible is the story of humans reaching out to God and God reaching out to humans. It's the story of how humans have tried through events, actions, poetry, prophecy and more to understand and connect with God, and of how God has sought to make himself known and understood by humans.'

There was a pause while that sunk in.

'I've never quite understood it that way,' I said, 'but I guess that is the common thread.' It's funny how people say things you probably already knew, but hadn't quite understood.

'Imagine reading a novel.' Easy for Ellie to do. She loves to read. 'The story includes descriptions of places and characters, a narrative of events, and a study of the characters — their conversations, thoughts and ideas, letters and messages. Some of it doesn't seem relevant at the time, but all of the elements help us to understand the characters and the events. It all comes together in one story. I read the Bible the same way. Each writer is adding their insights to the story, but it is one story.'

'I like reading the letters.'

'We know, Jo. You said that earlier.' Alex shook his head. 'And you like reading letters written to someone else? That's a worry.'

Jo pushed her hair back from her face. 'The letters in the New Testament were written by people with a genuine experience of Jesus. Peter and John were disciples and probably Jesus' closest friends; James was a brother of Jesus; Paul persecuted the early church until he had a personal experience of Jesus that blew his mind and change the entire course of his life. So the writers explain their understandings and beliefs. They try to teach the readers about the gospel and to guide the church, which often faced difficult situations. In trying to provide the clearest advice, they also include some opinions of their own about Christian behaviour, based on the culture of the time and the issues the reader was dealing with.'

'I like the fact that the letters acknowledge conflict,' said Mei. 'In the early years after Jesus, Christian churches sprang up in cities and towns where the dominant culture was hedonistic and commercial, so some Christians wanted to continue their old, corrupt life. And when Paul, in particular, tried to explain that this was inappropriate, they pushed back, using the familiar tactic of attacking him personally and trying to discredit his reputation and authority.'

'So there was inevitable conflict. What's your point?' Nathan was frowning.

'My point is that this is a PR nightmare. This is not the way to promote a cause. We would deal with the conflict behind closed doors, hoping that the emails and texts were not leaked while we prepared a press release that showed a united stand. Yet the Bible doesn't hide conflict; it doesn't conceal criticism; it doesn't try to get people's stories lined up before they get out. It is honest and real.'

'If many people wrote it, how can it be God's Word?' asked Arun.

'Well some Christians believe every word of the Bible explicitly. Others believe that it needs interpreting, with consideration of the time and place and socio-political context in which each book was written, and even with an understanding of who each author was. I personally don't believe God took the writer's hand and guided his pen across the page. I think each writer wrote his own thoughts and words. But I believe that God guided each writer so that he recorded God's truths. All Christians agree that it is God's Word because the writers were inspired and guided by God to write essential truths about God, truths that apply to all time and all places.'

'Well it was all written a long time ago, so it doesn't mean much now.' Nathan appeared to dismiss it.

'It does to me,' said Mei, 'because God's truths don't change.'

HEAVEN

Later still. Coffee? Sure. It will help me sleep.

'And what about heaven?' asked Arun.

'Pie in the sky when you die?' said Nathan.

'Ah,' said James.

'Because God loves us, when the time is right, he'll take us home — wherever that is.'

'Which is what we do with people we love,' suggested Ellie. 'Although I had some difficulty explaining Pete to my parents.'

I was surprised. 'I thought I charmed them.'

Ellie looked at the sky, rather dramatically, I thought. 'In your dreams.'

'No, that's where you were.' I thought that was a pretty good line. Ellie had no response. I barrelled on. 'And now Gabby has brought Arun home.'

Gabby blushed. 'Dad!'

'What?'

I don't really understand relationships. Fortunately James saved me from further gaffes.

'For Christians, faith is about this life and the next.'

'Will Alex be there?' Strange question, Nathan. Where is this going?

'I guess that's between God and Alex.'

'Hmmm. It won't be paradise if he's there.'

'If I'm there I'll give you hell!'

'Only joking, Alex. Although that's a confused metaphor, isn't it — giving me hell in heaven. Can that happen, James?'

'I don't think so, Nathan.'

'So we get pearly gates and streets of gold,' said Ani.

James brought some sanity to the interchange. 'The Bible is full of metaphors and we humans add our own bits to them. I don't know — or care — what heaven is like. I just know it will be good.'

'Probably plush carpet, good air conditioning and reliable internet connection. That would be heaven,' I suggested.

'The simple fact is that we cannot know what the after-life will be like,' said Mei. 'The closest we can come is to understand that we will be somehow closely connected to God, the source of all life, and that it will be awesome — in every sense of that word.'

'The Bible also talks about hell as the opposite of heaven.' Ellie was looking tired.

'Again,' said James, 'we have little idea what that will be like in reality, but we can assume that the opposite of a connection with God is alienation from God.'

'Christians are only ever dreaming about the next life.' I don't think we've convinced Nathan.

'Not at all. Jesus also promised a fulfilled life here and now, on earth.'

'When does that happen?'

'It already has.' He smiled and paused. 'For Christians, the promises of God are a fulfilled life on earth and something special after death. A fulfilled life doesn't mean a life of leisure and plenty — although some might experience that. It means that life has meaning and purpose. It is rewarding, not frustrating or pointless.'

'Sadly, many people believe that life is just a struggle, not enjoyable or meaningful, except in short flashes, and then it's over. We disappear into oblivion,' said Ellie.

'Perhaps we do,' said Ani. 'We can't prove it one way or another.'

'Of course. It's about personal belief. For myself, I don't know about the afterlife, and I don't much think about it, but, like James, I'm confident that it will be fine.'

'Even wonderful,' said Mei.

BECAUSE GOD IS GOD ... FAITH IS MORE THAN HOPING FOR MAGIC

Some people assume that faith is simply wishing and hoping that some magic will happen. Hope is a key element of Christianity, but it is not idle wishing.

Some deny that there is a God with the power to influence our lives, yet they believe that their health, happiness, wealth, relationships, employment, well-being and more can be influenced by movement of the stars, crystals, cards, or the colour and placement of their furniture.

Faith in God is not simply a wish that magic will happen. It is a confidence that God is who he says he is, that he will do what he has said he will do, that he cares about me as he has said he does, that I can have confidence in the future as he has said I can.

How can we understand this? How can we believe this? And what are the implications for our lives? What is God thinking?

It's simple really. God is God; we're not. He doesn't do magic; he does love.

Let me show you.

IN CHARGE

June 1: James and Mei's home. Same great company. Same great food. We really are lucky. Mei would say, 'God is good'.

Surprisingly, Arun and Gabby are here. Mei commented. 'I wasn't expecting you young folk to be here.'

'Should we go?' asked Gabby.

'Of course not.' Mei gave Gabby a hug. 'It's always great to have you here. You enliven the conversation.'

'And Arun asks a lot of questions — good questions.' Ellie gave him a hug. I think he's settling into the family.

'So why don't you go to church?' Gabby caught Arun off-guard, as she turned to look at him.

Arun was momentarily taken aback at the suddenness of the question, so took a moment to think. 'Er ...'

Gabby was apologetic. 'I'm sorry. I shouldn't have put you on the spot.'

'No, it's all right. It's a good question.' Arun took a breath. 'As a kid, I learned that if we ask God for anything in Jesus' name, he'll grant it, but it doesn't work. I have prayed for things and they haven't happened.'

'It got you a girlfriend.' I thought that was a good line.

'No, that was his good looks and natural charm.' An even better line, Gabby.

Arun smiled, before continuing. 'Joking aside, I prayed for my friend to get well; for the refugee crisis to be resolved; for a kid I know to not be bullied ... and none of it happened. What's the point? Is God even listening?'

'Ah,' said James.

'Because God is God, he doesn't attend job interviews or performance reviews. It's not really about what he can do for us; it's about what we can do for him. We don't call the shots; he does.'

'Eh? Isn't that a cop out?'

'Think about it.' James stroked his cheek. 'God is powerful, all-knowing, mysterious; he is beyond understanding; he is holy, set apart from humanity, and deserving of praise. Otherwise there is no point, because he is not God.' He paused. 'If we want God to meet our criteria, then we might as well stay with human demi-gods. God cannot be confined. He cannot be programmed like a robot. He's on the loose!'

'I recall that in the nineteen sixties, a popular movement claimed that God was dead — which is an oxymoron — because he didn't behave as people expected him to.' Mei looked at James. 'But, as James said, God is God. If he's accountable to us, then *we're* God and he's our servant. God is who he is. We don't make demands of him. He makes demands of us.'

'One of his demands is that *we* serve *him*,' said Jo.

'What's service?' Alex used his hands to add impact to the question. 'Servants are outdated.'

'To serve is simply to give our time and energy to meeting someone else's needs, or to do someone else's bidding.'

'Why does God want our service?' Alex persisted. 'He has the power to do everything for himself.'

'But we miss the point of faith,' said Jo. 'If we love, we put the loved one before ourselves. At its extreme, if we love, we are prepared to sacrifice whatever it takes for the one we love. So if we love God, if we accept all that God has done for us — as humanity and as an individual — then we will respond with service.'

'Jo's right,' said Ellie. 'For those we love we are happy to prepare a meal; collect them from work; help them with household chores; care for them when they are ill; hold them when they are afraid or anxious; buy them gifts that will make their lives easier or happier …'

I happened to be standing at the barbecue, moving the sausages around. It seemed appropriate to say, 'Because I love you, I give you the best sausage.' And I carried a sausage to her in the tongs and dropped it on her plate.

'Love is not a fluffy emotion,' said Jo. 'It's an active verb, a "doing" word; love is action. So it is with God. Our love for God is expressed as action.'

> So then, my friends, because of God's great mercy to us I appeal to you: Offer yourselves as a living sacrifice to God, dedicated to his service and pleasing to him. This is the true worship that you should offer. Do not conform yourselves to the standards of this world, but let God transform you inwardly by a complete change of your mind. Then you will be able to know the will of God — what is good and is pleasing to him and is perfect. (Romans 12: 1-3, NIV)

'Can I ask something?' asked Arun.

'You just did.' I thought it pretty obvious.

'Of course you can, Arun.' Ellie gave me an unappreciative glance. Well I was just stating the obvious, wasn't I?

'I don't know how to love God because I don't know him. How do I see him, talk to him, get to know him — or her?'

James said, 'We love God because of what he did for us. That's the Christian story. Jesus lived on earth as one of us, showed us how to live a fulfilling life; died a humiliating and painful death to pay for our sin and open the way to a relationship with a holy God; and came back to life to show that he had power even over death. And he didn't do it because we asked him to, but because, as we've been saying, he knows us, he loves us and he wants a relationship with us.'

'And we get to know him by spending time with him — chatting with him, listening to him through the Bible and our conversations with him, watching for the things he's doing around us and in us,' said Jo.

Gabby, who had been listening, now entered the conversation. 'I understand this. I want to serve God, but I don't really know how. I'm studying. I'm not about to run off to other parts of the world to help refugees and tell them about Jesus. So, how are we meant to serve him? How do we know what he wants us to do?' Good question, I thought, but I let James answer.

'Well, where you are is where you star,' said James.

Gabby frowned. 'What do you mean?'

'Put simply, we serve God wherever we happen to be at the time and using the opportunities we've been given. It's an easy out or a misunderstanding to say we would serve God if we were in a developing country, or if we had more money, or if we didn't have to go to work, or if we had a better education .... Where you are is where you star.'

'Although,' added Mei, 'Of course, we don't serve to God to win awards or applause. Perhaps we should say "No need to shift to use your gift."'

'I like that.' James nodded his approval. 'I stand corrected.'

'So what should I do?' asked Gabby.

'Well, firstly, go with what you know.' James stroked his eyebrow.

I interjected. 'When I think about Christian service, sometimes I feel like a mosquito at a nudist camp: I'm so overwhelmed by the possibilities I don't know where to start.' There was appreciative laughter, especially from Nathan, who almost fell off his chair. I didn't realise it was that funny.

'Spot on,' said James. 'We each have talents — music, writing, compassion, communication, empathy ... We each have learning and experience — administration, finance, bricklaying, maintenance, knitting, cooking, child care ... We each interact with people — at work, university, clubs, shops ... We serve using what we have and what we know among the people we interact with.'

Ellie said, 'So there are people at university who need to hear about God's love and need to see his love in action in practical ways.'

'But I'm no expert like you at preaching and I don't know the Bible like you do,' claimed Gabby. 'How can I talk about faith?'

'We grow in our understanding of faith as we live it and learn about it,' said Mei. 'But we can still share our own understanding.'

'How many ministers does it take to change a light bulb?' I asked, and paused long enough for comedic effect. 'Just one — because they are trained to bring light to a dark world.'

'I'm more likely to bring dark into a light world.' I hadn't realised how much Gabby was struggling with her own future.

Arun put his hand on hers. 'Not so, Gabs. You are full of light. That's one of the things I love about you. You just shine, even on days when things are tough or you're feeling down.' Gabby teared up, and as Arun put his arm around her, she put her head on his shoulder. I thought I was going to cry. Then Arun made sure I did by adding, 'Perhaps you've got more God in you than you think, Gabs.'

James saved the moment, before we all became emotional. 'Well, the ignition is mission.'

It was my turn to say, 'Eh?'

'What lights our fire for service? It is our love for God and our desire to share that love with others. It is our desire to build the church, telling people God's good news and helping Christians grow in faith. It is our love for the world and our passion to help others — for sharing God's love in practical ways with those who are part of our lives. This is the spark that gets our service motor started.'

'But what if I mess up and say something that actually puts people off God?' Gabby was still uncertain. 'Like people did with Nathan.'

Nathan wasn't expecting that, and he had no response.

James did. 'Well, we have recourse to God's resource.'

'Eh?'

'We may sometimes feel inadequate. At some time or other, I think each of us does. But the important thing is that when we serve God, we don't do it in our own strength. God works through us, and as he does that, he works in us, equipping us.'

'However, we should not be spiritually blasé about this.' I don't think Ellie is ever spiritually blasé. 'We need human support, too.'

'I agree,' said Jo. 'In the church, we support and encourage one another in service.'

Mei took a different tack. 'It's human nature for us to decide that some people's service is more important than others. The early church had to deal with it, and, even today, some people want to debate which gift, talent or experience is most valuable to God. But rather than a hierarchy of roles, I prefer to think of the hierarchy of the heart. That is, what matters more is our willingness, our commitment, whether we do what we do with a cheerful and willing heart. And that is available to anyone who serves God, no matter what their training or talent or opportunity.'

I thought that was a wonderful expression. 'I like that, Mei. "The hierarchy of the heart." Can I use that some time?'

'You may both quote it and live it.' That was clever too, I thought.

> *Because of God's gracious gift to me I say to every one of you: Do not think of yourself more highly than you should. Instead, be modest in your thinking, and judge yourself according to the amount of faith that God has given you. We have many parts in the one body, and all these parts have different functions. In the same way, though we are many, we are one body in union with Christ, and we are all joined to each other as different parts of one body. So we are to use our different gifts in*

> accordance with the grace that God has given us. If our gift is to speak God's message, we should do it according to the faith that we have; if it is to serve, we should serve; if it is to teach, we should teach; if it is to encourage others, we should do so. Whoever shares with others should do it generously; whoever has authority should work hard; whoever shows kindness to others should do it cheerfully. (Romans 12: 3-8, NIV)

'So how do I know if I'm doing any good?' asked Gabby.

'Well, what God needs is fruit with seeds,' replied James.

'Meaning?'

'In human organisations, our purpose is defined by results or outcomes or targets. If we achieve the measurable target, we have succeeded in our work, our service to the organisation or whoever it is we are accountable to. But the Bible consistently describes results as fruit.'

'What's your point, James?' Ani's question showed that she had been listening, even if not joining in. 'You forget my farming background. I know about fruit.'

'Then you'll understand that in nature, the fruit is not the end of the process; it is simply a part in the life cycle. If the fruit is good, it will produce good seeds, which in turn will produce more plants and more fruit.'

'That sounds like Nanna,' said Gabby. 'Lots of people talk about how she has helped them, and what a great role model as a Christian she is. And I don't think she'll ever stop, no matter how old she gets.'

'Well, the call is for all.' How does James keep coming up with these one-liners? 'It doesn't matter if we're a new Christian or a long-serving one, no matter what our talent or training or life experience, we are called to serve.'

'Even if we're old? Shouldn't Nanna rest and hand over to the next generation? Isn't it time she was served, instead of having to serve?'

'We should each take the test before we rest,' said James.

'What test?' I asked.

'Author Richard Bach wrote, "Here is a test to find whether your mission on Earth is finished. If you're alive it isn't."[2] That's true of our service for God. Of course we may pace ourselves more gently and our focus may change, but we continue to serve.'

'Why would we stop,' asked Mei, 'when we're serving a God who loves us?'

---

[2] The Bridge Across Forever: A True Love Story

MAKE IT COUNT

Later. Long conversation means much food has been consumed. So empty plates. Good coffee.

Nathan stood leaning on the back of a chair. 'That's all very interesting if you're religious, but I'm happy with my life, so I don't need it.'

'Ah,' said James.

'Because God is God, he wants our lives to count for something. After all, we're all religious, although "spiritual" may be a better word. God made us all that way.'

Nathan was not convinced. '*I'm* not religious.'

'Every person on the planet is religious.' James scratched under both ears simultaneously. 'Religion is a framework of beliefs that gives a purpose to our lives. Every one of us has something that defines who we are and what we believe and what matters most to us — even if we have never consciously defined it. For example, it may be money. If most of your thinking and decisions and actions are directed towards accumulating wealth, then perhaps your goal in life is to be as wealthy as you can.'

'I'm a vet,' said Nathan. 'My purpose is making unhappy animals happy.'

'I'm a courier,' said Alex, 'but that's a job, not my purpose in life.'

'What is?' asked Nathan.

'I've never thought about it. Probably just to be a decent bloke, be kind and helpful to people.'

'The problem is that when our belief is in ourselves and our abilities, or in money or pleasure or another person, we are bound to be let down. With God, we are never let down.' Mei speaks with such assurance.

Jo agreed with her. 'When your purpose is to serve God, to honour him in all of your relationships and activities, to use Jesus as a model for your life, you can never be let down.'

'Everyone's life has a purpose,' said James, 'a goal or focus which drives us. Our time, energy and money are directed towards achieving that goal. The leaders or role models or heroes we follow focus our attention on that goal. Because God is God, our core purpose in life ought to be to serve him. It may take us to unexpected places, bring us unanticipated joy and fill our life with unrivalled meaning.'

Mei added, 'If you choose to serve God, your life will count for something. He'll make sure of it. People will be different because of you. The world will be different because of you — even though you may not know it!'

CONCLUSION

Later. But never too late.

'So that's God's message,' said James, 'evident in his actions: He knows us. That means he knows you. He wants a relationship with us. That means he wants a relationship with you. He loves us. That means he loves you. But he is God and that has implications for us. That means it has implications for you.'

'How do you deal with that?' asked Arun.

'You simply respond. You say to God, "Loving Father, here I am talking to you, the Creator of the Universe. I love a good mystery, but this one baffles me: That in Jesus, you shared our humanity; that you know this humanity you created, and that you know me; that you want a relationship with me; that you love me; that there is no impediment to this relationship except the walls that I create. Yet this is what I want to believe. So, Father, come into my heart. Fill me with your Spirit, not just in the spare nooks and crannies of my life, but in the core of my being. Live in me, so that I experience a life enriched and fulfilled in you."'

'And if you have experienced this life of faith,' he continued, 'if you know you are loved by God and try to live for him each day, you might say, "Loving Father, come into my heart anew. I've crammed too much into my life and into my heart. I've lost track of what really matters. Push some of this stuff out so that there is room for your Spirit to expand and thrive in my life."'

'And who knows where he will take us,' said Mei.

'Or why? Because God knows us, wants a relationship with us, loves us, then …' James simply raised his eyebrows and smiled, the sentence left unfinished.

By the same author:

Reflections on faith inspired by children
Reflections on faith inspired by seniors
Reflections on faith inspired by men
Reflections on faith inspired by babies
Reflections on faith inspired by COVID
Faith around the barbecue (The play)

Go to **www.philridden.biz**

www.ingramcontent.com/pod-product-compliance
Lightning Source LLC
Chambersburg PA
CBHW070307010526
44107CB00056B/2509